GENTLEMEN
TO THE RESCUE

BY THE SAME AUTHOR

Continued Next Week
World of Laughter
Kops and Custards
Bound and Gagged
Clown Princes and Court Jesters
Collecting Classic Films
Winners of the West
Dreams for Sale
Ladies in Distress
Mack Sennett's Keystone
Collecting Vintage Cameras
Glass, Brass & Chrome

GENTLEMEN
TO THE RESCUE

The Heroes of the Silent Screen

Kalton C. Lahue

CASTLE BOOKS ★ **NEW YORK**

Printed in the United States of America

CONTENTS

INTRODUCTION

As I write this, I've just finished editing a large amount of prehistorical films from the Kinetoscope and Mutoscope days of 1893–1900, which reaffirm a long-held suspicion that even without its "Ladies in Distress," the silent screen could have easily survived on the exploits of its numerous heroes alone. While the ladies were and are important to the motion picture, the appeal of the heroes should not be underestimated. They were a small, select breed, many of whom outlasted their feminine counterparts in popularity; that fact alone accounts for the smaller number of favorites included between the covers of this volume than in my previous *Ladies in Distress.*

The ladies had an appeal of their own (today we call it sex), but time and age took its toll on their careers; only a talented few like Lillian Gish surmounted this liability. It was a different story with the men, except those who were already well into their prime when they came to the movies. The life expectancy of a male hero was considerable, providing that he watched the roles he played and for whom he worked. Those who stayed within the bounds of the major studios could look forward to an undarkened future. The only roadblock was an unforeseen one: the advent of the talkies. They did damage the careers of many.

The heroic male image appealed to both male and female filmgoers, and especially to those of us young enough to be rudely referred to by agitated theatre managers as "damn kids." In today's world, there's a desperate lack of heroes with whom the young can identify; many are even anti-heroic, and those of us who are older were indeed fortunate. It may have been a world of black and white, good and bad, but at least the direction in which our heroes pointed us was a clear-cut path. And it's certainly true that when we became a little older we learned about the many shades of grey between the two extremes, and that virtue by itself was small reward; but by then, most of us were quite capable of coping with the realities of life around us.

The experiences may not have been so mind-expanding as those enjoyed by some of our younger generation of today, but then the hangovers were few and far between.

There are those who maintain that the young should model themselves on the real world; thank heaven for idealism, but why confuse the issue? While some would disagree, it can be fairly said, I think, that we didn't do so badly modeling ourselves on the fantasy world of Milton Sills, Tommy Meighan and Doug Fairbanks. They were winners then and the basic forces that motivated their screen images would make them winners today—times haven't changed that much. And just to prove that point, I offer the reader thirty examples in the pages ahead.

They may not be the exact thirty you would have selected, but taken as an entity, they represent the wide range of heroes that scampered across the screen in an era that seems refreshingly uncomplicated today. If I have left out a favorite of yours, please bear with me—it does not mean that I think him unimportant, but only that space limitations preclude attempting to satisfy everyone.

My thanks to the many film collectors and individuals who made this volume possible and special thanks for the unusual illustrations should be given the Academy of Motion Picture Arts and Sciences, Larry Edmunds Bookshop, John Hampton's Silent Movie Theatre, John Doughty of Blackhawk Films and the National Film Archives, British Film Institute, who assisted in my attempt to assemble illustrations which are representative of each actor while avoiding those commonly in use.

GENTLEMEN
TO THE RESCUE

KING BAGGOT

It's a great shame that so little of the film's early years have been preserved. While much of what passed across the screen during that time was hardly art, it did constitute a social document; and once a method of preserving the real world had come to pass, it was an unpardonable sin that so few felt it worth retaining. As it stands, much of the work of pioneer actors, actresses and directors has taken its place in the myths of film history and the intensive searches now being mounted for these films will turn up only a small portion; the rest seem destined to remain a part of a legend beyond verification.

One of the most popular of the early stars was an actor in a St. Louis stock company who finally arrived on Broadway but left the stage in 1909 to become one of the "flicker folk" in an era when motion picture actors were considered even less respectable than those who toured the country in traveling stock companies. King Baggot joined Carl Laemmle's IMP that year to begin a career that would last until only a few months before his death in 1948. One of the more talented players to join the independent ranks, Baggot's roles in *The Scarlet Letter, Dr. Jekyll and Mr. Hyde* and *Shamus O'Brien* soon placed him high in the ranks of popular favorites.

When Laemmle spirited Florence Lawrence away from Biograph in 1910, it was King Baggot who escorted her to St. Louis, where a crowd of fans enthusiastically greeted them at the station in what proved to be the first personal appearance tour. Of course, it was Miss Lawrence who was physically mauled by the crowd, which chose to demonstrate its affection by tearing buttons, trimmings and whatever else they could from her person as a souvenir, but Baggot came in for his share of attention from the mob.

Thirty years old when he came to the screen, Baggot's career as a leading man reached its climax with his portrayal of *Ivanhoe* in 1913. The star had accompanied director Herbert Brenon and cast to the town of Chepstow, England, where a castle had been leased for the month of

July. Filming attracted residents from as far away as Bristol to watch this dramatic re-creation of English history in three reels, and Baggot received their applause for the energy and showmanship he put into each scene. It was almost as much fun as appearing on the live stage once more. *Ivanhoe's* release in September brought considerable acclaim to Universal, whose great fame as an assembly line of program pictures was just beginning.

Toward the close of his starring career, King Baggot left Universal to appear in two serial cliffhangers—*The Eagle's Eye* and *The Hawk's Trail*—both of which allowed him to indulge in his favorite pastime of playing multiple roles. Almost from the start of his career, Baggot loved to don makeup and play as many parts as possible. He had carried this to its logical conclusion in 1914 when he carried the entire two reels of *Shadows* by himself, playing the mother, her son, the uncle, a merchant, Chinese servant, prostitute, jailor, villain, police officer and detective, with two or more of these characters appearing on-screen at the same time. This tour de force was repeated in *The Hawk's Trail,* with Baggot giving ten characterizations—but older and wiser, he allowed Grace Darmond and Rhea Mitchell to play themselves. Of course, silent screen makeup wasn't nearly as good as that later used by Lon Chaney and the alert viewer had little trouble picking out the hero regardless of the disguise, but it was a first (and a last) in serial history.

By the early twenties, King Baggot was in his forties and leading roles were now few and far between. After a few supporting roles, he signed a long-time contract with Universal as a director, and while his best known effort behind the megaphone was coincidentally Bill Hart's final western (*Tumbleweeds,* 1925), Baggot turned out creditable program pictures into the sound era. When directing jobs became scarce, he went to work with a pencil and turned up as a script writer, a talent he had exercised as early as 1913. Unlike so many of his contemporaries who felt completely lost once their glory began to fade, survival was a fun kind of challenge to King Baggot, whose confidence in his own abilities was far too great to allow dismal reflection on what might have been.

While very little of Baggot's starring work is known to exist at the present time, it's fortunate that a print of *Ivanhoe* is available; and while the pageantry and pomp as portrayed in 1913 seems just a bit strained and artificial today, the talent of King Baggot comes across with ease; it's not hard to see why he was one of the screen's earliest favorites.

King Baggot.

Ivanhoe, *1913.*

King bids Jane Fearnley goodbye in King the Detective and the Smugglers, *a 1912 Imp. Baggot dearly loved detective roles, especially those which allowed him to perform in disguise.*

Ethel Grandin and Baggot in Love Versus Law, *a 1913 drama about a man who tried to impress his girl and landed in jail for his trouble. The ending? The real bandit stepped forward like a good sport and his confession set King free.*

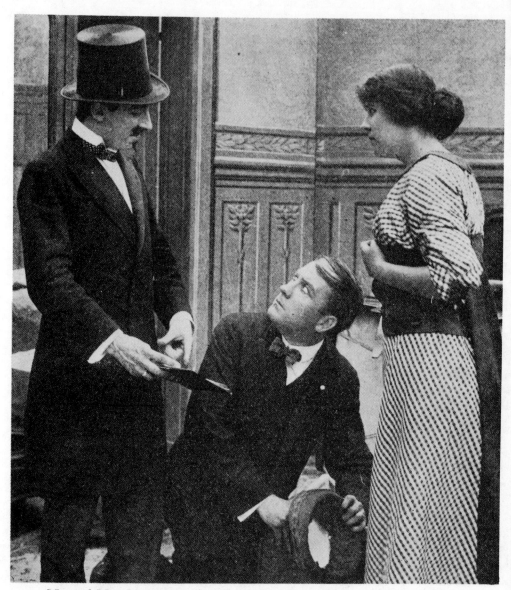

Mr. and Mrs. Innocence Abroad *detailed the adventures of King Baggot and Leah Baird on a trip to Paris. Made during the trip to England where Ivanhoe was filmed, it was one of those little "fillers" that moviemakers used to help amortize their costs.*

JOHN BARRYMORE

Few men conquered the mediums of stage and screen more thoroughly than John Barrymore. In a career that spanned more years than he once cared to recall, Barrymore delivered some of the most electrifying performances ever put on celluloid, especially in those roles calling for the bizarre, or even more to his liking, the grotesque. No one has ever duplicated his amazing portrayal in *Dr. Jekyll and Mr. Hyde* nor that of his Captain Ahab in *The Sea Beast*. A completely professional actor with command of a wide and varied pantomimic range, he played every possible role from light comedy and romantic nonsense to the deepest of drama, but John Barrymore was at his best when the role called for a warped mind or deformed body. He seemed to absolutely delight in such performances, and if the script did not provide him with an opportunity to display his marvelous talent, John would deftly arrange for at least a sequence that allowed him a disguise or a moment of madness.

The public remembers Barrymore as a great lover, and although he *was* in roles like *Beau Brummell,* he was also much more—a sensitive and demanding individual who failed to become a top box-office attraction. His association with the stage, his famous name and the expensively produced Paramount and Warner features in which he starred in the twenties combined with his choice of roles to keep the era's greatest actor from becoming the screen's top star. The ladies preferred him in romantic nonsense, men were unable to understand how such a dandy had made it so far in life, and rural audiences didn't care at all. But scattered across the country there were a sufficient number who appreciated Barrymore to keep his screen career bright; and with the number of off-screen escapades in which John was involved furnishing a large store of delightful stories for gossip columnists, Barrymore attracted more than his share of curiosity seekers wondering what he had besides talent, looks and money—all things they seemed to lack. Every marital mishap was recounted in full measure and the star's sharp wit and vivid way with unquotable language kept him front page news.

Barrymore had started on-screen during World War I with a series of light comedies that soon gave way to dramatic fare like *Raffles,* but it was his *Dr. Jekyll and Mr. Hyde* that brought John nationwide attention. Scorning the extensive makeup used by James Cruze and Sheldon Lewis (as well as later actors who repeated the role) in their versions of the Robert Louis Stevenson story, John did most of the transformation by muscular control, and as Lon Chaney could twist and contort his body into a variety of deformities, John Barrymore could feign madness with ease. The absolute delight with which the star approached such a scene proved to be the high point of filming for the crew—it was like working with a genuine madman.

Many have accused Barrymore of being a ham who loved the limelight, and they are right to an extent; all successful actors need a touch of this trait to make them function, but to John's credit he never went overboard on-screen. He knew that he was a star, no one had to remind him of this or constantly boost his ego; for Barrymore also realized that he was an actor and one of the best. His family heritage had given John a sincere love and respect for his profession. He found the challenge not in the paycheck but in the role itself; Barrymore would have and occasionally did perform for a pittance if the role intrigued him.

Interesting parts in films that varied from good to bad came his way in the twenties: *Tempest, Beau Brummell, When a Man Loves, Sherlock Holmes, The Beloved Rogue* and others. If some of these had no other redeeming qualities, they did contain superb performances by the star that many modern actors would do well to study. Like Chaplin in the art of comedy, Barrymore's acting was devoted to the minutiae of pantomime—small gestures, raised eyebrows, graceful flourishes of head and hand, minute expression changes—all combining to convince the viewer that John was really living the moment on-screen and not acting at all.

John Barrymore easily adapted himself to the sound era. Now his well-trained stage voice could be heard and the full dimension of "The Great Profile" could be appreciated by ear as well as eye. Barrymore continued to give sterling performances in roles like *Svengali* and *Arsene Lupin,* but as the thirties wore on, his personal problems (which had always been great) began to overshadow the professional life. Plagued by alcoholism and women, he ended his career in B mysteries, supporting roles and a parody of himself, *The Great Profile.* Wild spending sprees, income taxes and alimony ate up his vast financial resources (Barrymore always lived extremely well) and by his death in 1942, the actor was adjudged bankrupt.

The tragedy of John Barrymore's life was recorded at length by his friend Gene Fowler in *Goodnight Sweet Prince,* a biography written shortly after his death. That such talent should come to so humble an end is sad, but at least some of Barrymore's finer moments were preserved on film. It's always a wondrous experience to fade a half-century into the past and watch John Barrymore in his prime as he re-creates man's internal struggles with himself, the very failing to which the great actor finally succumbed.

John Barrymore.

Barrymore in one of his early Paramount roles as The Lost Bridegroom, 1916.

As Dr. Jekyll and Mr. Hyde, *with Louis Wolheim, in a 1920 performance yet to be surpassed.*

Barrymore relaxes with a cigarette while discussing the next scene with director Alan Crosland and writer Bess Meridyth between takes on the set of Don Juan, 1926.

John gave a spirited performance as the vagabond poet Francois Villon in 1927's The Beloved Rogue. *Slim Summerville as Jehan and Mack Swain as Nicholas added to the gaiety of this scene.*

Barrymore delighted in portraying characters like Captain Ahab in The
Sea Beast, *1926.*

The Great Garbo and The Great Profile in Grand Hotel, 1932.

RICHARD BARTHELMESS

Richard Barthelmess's rise to screen fame came rather quickly, but unlike others whose star ascended rapidly, his popularity did not fade as the years passed. While his best roles had come early in his career, an occasional story passed Dick's way in the twenties that served to rejuvenate his career, and Barthelmess had no difficulty carrying on into talkies with a large following of fans. The son of a wealthy importer and an actress, Barthelmess was a New Yorker whose youth was quite comfortable financially. In 1913 he enrolled in Hartford's Trinity College. During his summer vacation two years later, Dick decided to indulge a taste for dramatics as a member of the Hartford Film Corporation, a newly formed organization that had high hopes of turning the wilds of Connecticut into another Hollywood. As might be expected, the corporation went bankrupt within a few weeks and Barthelmess spent the rest of the summer working with the Travelers Insurance Company before returning to college in the fall. It may not have been a very profitable summer, but it was an exciting one, and it gave the young man an idea.

After another year at Trinity, Dick went back to New York City for the summer where he managed to land work as an extra in *Gloria's Romance,* Billie Burke's one fling at a movie serial. This convinced him that pictures offered a good career, and through his mother, Dick gained an interview with Nazimova, who was about to begin filming *War Brides,* her 1916 melodrama of the European conflict. Nazimova introduced him to Herbert Brenon, and the director agreed to give the young man a small role at $7.50 daily. Brenon took such a liking to the young actor that when he left Selznick the director put Barthelmess under personal contract at $50 weekly.

To this point, Dick Barthelmess was just another good-looking, masculine personality with little about him to suggest his soon-to-arrive popularity. But a chance meeting with D. W. Griffith paved the way. Lillian Gish had ventured the opinion that Barthelmess was too short to work with her, but it all came to pass in a most unusual way. Griffith was casting for *Broken Blossoms,* with stand-ins working in the roles not yet selected. George Fawcett filled in for the Chinese lad who was to save Miss Gish from her unmentionable fate at the hands of Donald Crisp and Barthelmess watched him rehearse. Fawcett was far too old for the role, but he had worked under Griffith for years and knew exactly what the director was looking for in the portrayal. Barthelmess watched Fawcett closely and when he was given the opportunity to test for the role, cleverly assumed the part as Fawcett had played it and Griffith chose him for the lead.

A huge hit for its time, this exquisite melodrama was capped by a sensitive performance by Barthelmess and a superb one by Miss Gish. Dick attained stardom with this one role. His virile masculinity was in sharp contrast to that of Griffith's other leading men, especially little Robert Harron, a fine actor but one whose physical appearance restricted the type of roles he could play. Barthelmess continued working under Griffith, playing the lead in *Way Down East* when good fortune crossed his path once again.

Griffith had bought screen rights to several works of author Joseph Hergesheimer and among the lot was a short story, *The Happy End.* The director had little real intention of filming it, but the story caught Barthelmess's eye, and he approached D. W. about the possibility of buying the property. Always pressed for cash, D. W. put a $125,000 price tag on it and Barthelmess went out in search of a loan. He found it in the person of financier Averell Harriman, who offered to put up the money on a star-story basis; Barthelmess would found Inspiration Pictures and star in the resulting film. Dick adapted much of the story to the screen by himself and then hired as his director Henry King, a former actor who had turned out competent but unspectacular work to that time.

Tol'able David (1921) was one of the high points of the year and a milestone both in the cinema and Barthelmess's career. Its absolute success guaranteed the future of Dick's company and the uncomplicated story of a mountain lad whose fondest dream was to deliver the mail, a position entrusted to his elder brother, won him a flock of fans. Melodrama was introduced in the person of Ernest Torrance as the leader of the Hatburns, a sadistic trio of outlaws on the run who crippled David's brother and killed his father. His mother stifled the boy's impulse for revenge, and when eventually entrusted with the mail, David was also attacked by the Hatburns. In a savagely realistic fight sequence, the star won out over the outlaws and delivered the mail.

Moving leisurely most of the time, the story was a well-directed piece of Americana with superb photography and a strong portrayal by Barthelmess. It remains as one of the last filmed representations of a vanishing rural America; a remake a decade later failed to capture the same spirit as the original (the inevitable fate of most attempts to redo a classic picture) and seen today, *Tol'able David* is perhaps even more moving for those who realize that the past, while prologue, can never be recaptured.

Barthelmess and his Inspiration Pictures went on to film 11 more stories in the next five years, all of which were released by First National and all of which made money. They had entertainment as their prime purpose but none rose to the heights of *Tol'able David*. Only in *Soul Fire* did Dick come close to repeating his performance, this time as a composer whose concerto was accompanied by flashbacks portraying the events in his life that represented the inspiration for each movement.

First National offered Barthelmess a contract in 1927 calling for three pictures a year at a salary of $375,000 each, and the actor reluctantly disbanded his company. He was to express regret at the move in later years, for production had overtaken acting as his first love, but at the time the financial arrangements were too good to pass up. *The Patent Leather Kid* came along about this time and once more Barthelmess's fans stormed to box-offices to watch their favorite as an unpopular East side boxer who knew no fear in the ring, but whose cowardly nature appeared when he was drafted to go to war. As with all good endings, Dick overcame his fear when his buddy was killed and fought like a demon to win his girl and overcome the wounds that heroism had brought him—audiences weeped unashamedly.

Barthelmess had no difficulties with talkies and *The Dawn Patrol* in 1930 reaffirmed his popularity once again. His screen personality varied only slightly over the years despite occasional roles as a heavy. Dick retired from the screen in 1941 a millionaire and still a star with 76 pictures to his credit. He turned down several offers to return to movies over the years and remained in retirement until his death a few years ago. Enduring fame had come has way early and he felt no compelling need to reaffirm it—*Broken Blossoms, Tol'able David, The Patent Leather Kid* and *The Dawn Patrol*—a decade of hits and a permanent niche in the screen's history. What could he have accomplished by a comeback?

Richard Barthelmess.

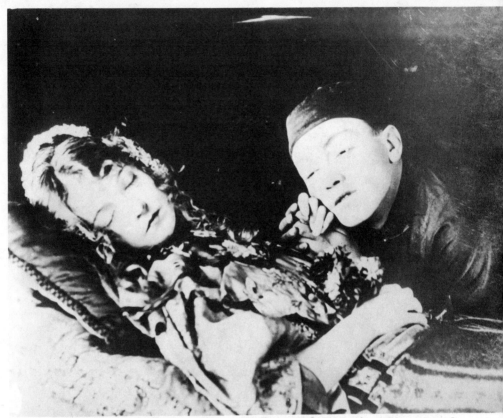

As the Chinese boy who protected Lillian Gish in Broken Blossoms, *the 1919 role that brought Barthelmess acclaim.*

With Miss Gish once again in Way Down East, 1920. *Barthelmess would soon leave Griffith and start his own company, Inspiration Pictures.*

Tol'able David *was the first script filmed by Barthelmess under his In-spiration Pictures banner and remains his best-known role. That's Gladys Hulett in the background.*

The Enchanted Cottage, *1924.*

Dick Barthelmess at home in the early twenties.

Barthelmess and Bessie Love in Soul Fire, *1925.*

The Patent Leather Kid *reports to duty, 1927.*

As the condemned man in The Noose, *1928.*

A moment of high drama in The Dawn Patrol, *1930.*

The Lash, *a 1930 talkie.*

Barthelmess began to show his age in Heroes for Sale, 1933.

CARLYLE BLACKWELL

There were a number of the early screen actors you just couldn't help liking, regardless of their talent. A few possessed an engaging screen personality that made their acting superfluous, while others were so striking in physical appearance that they seemed to fit every part in which they were cast. If an actor could lay claim to the personality and the appearance, and if he was fortunate enough to have ability in addition, he, like Carlyle Blackwell, was bound to be rewarded for his cinematic endeavors.

A native of Syracuse, New York, enrolled at Cornell, Blackwell came to the movies through an unfortunate disagreement with his father. The younger Blackwell had spent his summers in New York's Catskills, providing entertainment for the tourists who spent their vacations at the resorts and he wanted to become an actor. Worried about his son's future, dad wanted him to study something substantial, like engineering. The two came to a resolution of this problem when Carlyle was 19— as dad was paying the bills, the son would leave school.

Carlyle headed for Denver, where he joined Elich's Stock Company; one year later he had worked his way to New York City, where he signed with the Keith-Proctor Stock Company. After playing a number of juvenile roles, he made the jump to Broadway, and by 1910, was slowly building a reputation as a stage actor. But as the theatrical bug had bitten him several years before, he now began to seriously consider the infant motion picture industry. While older actors scoffed at the movies, Carlyle was certain that a far greater future rested in the celluloid strips than on the stage, and in 1910 he made the break, joining Vitagraph at its Flatbush studio where he again played juvenile parts. Eight months passed and Carlyle was seen in dozens of Vitagraph films; but very little developed as a result of his move, other than a steady paycheck. George Melford had noticed the young actor and Blackwell accepted his offer of a higher salary to become a member of the Kalem Company's player roster.

Carlyle spent a little over three years with Kalem, and once more he played in every conceivable role, from western to costume drama and even light comedy, but now they were leading roles opposite actresses like Alice Joyce. While his magnetic personality and striking good looks were his strongest assets, Blackwell also made progress as an actor, acquiring a following of fans as well as a nickname. In recognition of his ability to start a two-reeler in the morning and complete it before quitting for the day, coworkers referred to Carlyle as "Picture-a-day" Blackwell.

But our hero had now concluded that his future rested not in acting but production, and accordingly he established his own company, arranging for release through the International Film Service, soon to become a part of Pathé. Although he turned out some interesting pictures, the move proved to be one huge mistake, as Blackwell not only owned the company, but also managed its affairs, directed its production activities and starred in his own films. The entire arrangement turned out to be far too much for one man to handle successfully, especially since he regarded his reputation of man about town and romantic idol as one that should not be overlooked during off-hours.

Carlyle was not the playboy type; he just believed in enjoying himself and so 1915 found him back in harness at Lasky, where he was one of the first actors to draw a salary of $2000 weekly—not a bad sum for a kid who had quit college to avoid a career as an engineer. World Films offered him a contract as leading man soon after he had joined Lasky, and from 1915 to 1919 Carlyle Blackwell appeared on the screen under the World banner in a long series of dramas. Leaving World for Paramount, Blackwell spent three years there and then quit the industry in 1922 to move abroad. Settling in England, he turned up as a corporate officer of Gainsborough Films in London and functioned as an actor, director and producer for 14 years. From this period came the one film for which he's best remembered today—a screen translation of Sir Henry Rider Haggard's popular novel *She,* produced by G. B. Samuelson during 1925 and released on the independent market in this country in 1926.

She adhered to Haggard's novel quite faithfully and starred Betty Blythe, best known for her 1921 *Queen of Sheba,* in the "title" role, with Blackwell playing the descendant of her lover who fell under her immortal spell. The film created little attention in the United States when it was released, yet over the years it has remained in popular folklore as a picture to be seen. Carlyle had little to do in *She* except to clench his jaw firmly, so the film can hardly be said to represent the actor at his best, yet *She* is one of his few leading roles available at this time.

Carlyle Blackwell has been credited as the man who gave Alfred Hitchcock his chance to direct in England and if for no other reason, all Hitchcock fans will agree that this was an important contribution to the movies. Blackwell returned to this country and settled in Miami, where he resided until his death in 1955. Never one of the great stars of the silents, he could and should have been, but an independent will kept him from succumbing to that overpowering urge to push his way into the upper ranks and stay there. Carlyle Blackwell was one of those few screen actors to whom a good performance was sufficient, and as long as his fans were happy, so was he.

A Dixie Mother, *1910.*

Carlyle Blackwell and Neva Gerber in The High Hand, *1914.*

With Doris Kenyon in The Ocean Waif, *1914.*

Blackwell had aged considerably when She *was produced in 1925 but the same grim determination flashed from his eyes.*

FRANCIS X. BUSHMAN

When one thinks of the silent screen and the aura of romance that accompanies its brief span, the name Francis X. Bushman majestically rises up with all the splendor of a near-legend. Although he wasn't the first of the matinee idols (Bushman came just a bit later than Maurice Costello), he certainly was the most enduring, and his on-screen romance with Beverly Bayne during the World War I years had just as much impact as the later and more publicized Gilbert-Garbo affair.

Fans tend to remember Bushman first for his portrayal of Messala in *Ben Hur* and secondly for the increase in blood pressure and heart beat caused by his strikingly handsome profile as he took Miss Bayne into his arms in countless romantic clinches. As the two images are worlds apart, this is somewhat of a paradox, but there's little doubt that it was the role in *Ben Hur* that contributed heavily toward his minor legend and capped a career that otherwise might have simply faded quietly.

A native of Norfolk, Virginia, Francis Xavier Bushman was educated at Ammendale College in Maryland, and among other things had been a wrestler, bicycle racer, model for artists and sculptors and actor in various repertoire and stock companies when he joined the Essanay Company at its Chicago studio in 1911. When *The Ladies' World* invited its readers to choose their personal screen favorites three years later, Bushman's votes overwhelmed ranking favorite Costello and a new champion took his place.

Dashingly handsome, Bushman possessed a youthful and attractive physique and Essanay made the most of both attributes by frequently casting him in costume dramas like *Under Royal Patronage* and *Graustark* —roles that took advantage of his splendid build and regal appearance in uniforms. Equally at home in top hat and tails, he was appealing in society dramas, and demonstrating a flair for drawing room humor, he also made numerous light-hearted comedies.

Bushman reigned supreme at Essanay until the company insisted that he support Viola Allen in her screen debut. This affront could not be accepted by the star, whose one outstanding fault was also an admirable trait; he felt that his integrity as an actor was being compromised. This sense of integrity would later keep him from the screen for several years, but in 1915 Bushman had another option and he exercised it—he and Miss Bayne moved over to Metro to continue their great success for Louis B. Mayer. When the star managed to obtain a divorce from his wife—a marriage carefully concealed from fans by both Essanay and Metro, who had feared that audiences would spurn him had they known of his wife and several children—he and Miss Bayne were quietly married in a ceremony which was also kept from the public on the assumption that watching husband and wife make love on-screen as they had in *Romeo and Juliet* (1918) would ruin the illusion of a great romantic affair.

Bushman and Bayne were a mainstay of the newly formed Metro Company, as they had been at Essanay, and brought untold sums of wealth into the organization's coffers by playing in everything from comedy and drama to a serial, *The Great Secret.* The latter proved to be a financial white elephant, as chapter play fans liked action instead of romance and the duo's fans were not fond of the idea of following a story that was revealed only a little at a time each week. But these years were good ones for the two, who had become so inextricably bound together in the public mind that one was not referred to without the other. And it was during these closing years of what one popular historian has termed as "America's last great fling with romanticism" that Bushman and Bayne reigned supreme.

By the early twenties, their type of screen fare was fast losing its vogue and the screen's first great romantic team returned to the stage. In 1923, Bushman came back to Hollywood and formed FXB Pictures to film *Modern Marriage,* then was offered the role as Massala in *Ben Hur,* which was being prepared for the camera. He called William S. Hart to ask his advice (Hart had played both Messala and Ben Hur on the stage) and Hart assured him that Messala was the desired role. Bushman then proposed that Rudolph Valentino play Ben Hur, but the role was given to George Walsh.

In 1924, the distinguished actor accompanied the huge crew abroad where he learned that it would be months before his role was to be filmed. Despite numerous cast and crew changes, which saw Ramon Novarro replace Walsh as Ben Hur, Bushman stuck it out, only to be severely reprimanded by Mayer for trying to "upstage" the newcomer Novarro on-screen. Even though *Ben Hur* and Francis X. Bushman were acclaimed as a critical and popular hit, producers failed to rush to his door and Bushman found it necessary to return to the stage late in the twenties; some say that Mayer paid back the man who had helped Metro so much in its early days by trying to keep him from the screen.

Bushman's sense of integrity kept him from exploiting his name and reputation for a fast dollar, and although he was occasionally seen on the screen almost until his death a few years ago, it was only toward the end that he finally succumbed and undertook roles in such ridiculous fare as the American International *Bikini Party* and horror film cycles of the sixties. To his credit, Bushman managed to bring a sense of dignity even to those bits—about all the worth the pictures really had.

But how often he must have thought back to those few years when he was young, and the screen belonged to Francis X. Bushman and Beverly Bayne; he had felt deeply that movies would come of age to be a great educational and morally uplifting force, but then, who in 1920 could have predicted that the best picture of a half-century later (if the Academy Awards mean anything at all) would revolve around the story of a homosexual and a male hustler?

Bushman and Bayne in The Power of Conscience, *1914.*

Francis X. Bushman, circa 1918.

Audiences watching the screen's first great love duo were unaware that Bushman was married and had a family. When he wed Beverly Bayne after his divorce, that fact was also concealed from their adoring public.

A Pair of Cupids, *1918.*

Bushman did as well with light comedy roles as with romantic scenes and heavy drama.

One of the most famous confrontations in screen history—Ramon Novarro as Ben Hur *meets his antagonist* Messala. *This 1927 role was Bushman's best part in many years.*

LON CHANEY

George Loane Tucker's The Miracle Man was quite a picture. Although hokey in the best sense of the word, this melodramatic offering of 1919 brought Tommy Meighan and Lon Chaney to stardom at the same time. Chaney was most deserving of the reward; he had spent several years laboring on the screen in near-obscurity. Sadly, his greatest fame was to come not so much by virtue of the man's considerable talents as from the types of grotesque creatures which he played on-screen, a circumstance that somewhat later afflicted another struggling actor named Boris Karloff after he was chosen to be encased in the makeup of the Frankenstein monster in the early thirties.

Born of deafmute parents, young Chaney learned at an early age how to communicate via sign language and pantomime, a technique that years on the stage had perfected along with the art of makeup. Early Hollywood studios had no makeup men and actors were required to apply their own with whatever degree of skill they possessed. When Chaney tried the movies, he found that the small box constantly by his side proved the most certain avenue through studio gates. He could easily and quickly turn himself into an old man, a sailor or anything else the director desired. Gradually, he worked up to leading roles in a few Universal two-reelers around 1915, but Lon wasn't a handsome man and scripts seldom called for leading actors who weren't attractive to women.

But perseverance and talent eventually won out, and in 1919 he was cast as the cripple in *The Miracle Man,* a role that required he drag himself along without the use of legs until the charlatan who "cured" him could work the "miracle," as a part of a successful confidence game. The sense of utter desperation that Chaney brought to this role, and his apparent overcoming of futility by sheer willpower brought him to public notice. Lon suddenly found himself in demand for more challenging parts, as today's Academy Award winners find their salaries boosted by one of the small golden Oscars.

The greatest fame was yet to come; there were still trite roles to be played but now at least they were leading ones. As the Chinaman of *Shadows,* the French-Canadian backwoodsman of *Nomads of the North* and the hired killer of *The Shock,* Lon Chaney brought a depth and sensitivity to the screen that far exceeded the value of the scripts. There was much personal tragedy in his life, and like a tortured soul's window to the world, Chaney's eyes mirrored the sadness of real life to the screen audiences.

He was especially effective in *The Shock* as the gunman who fell in love with his intended victim's daughter. Using a wheelchair as the ruse that allowed him close contact to his victim without suspicion, Chaney soon fell in love with the sympathetic daughter. Unable to accomplish his mission, Chaney became a marked man, but his life and love was saved by the San Francisco earthquake, which disposed of the criminal gang to which he belonged. Chaney's change of character was slow but quite evident, as if he were leading the audience by the hand as he passed from a life of evil to one of charity and kindness.

In 1923, he undertook the role of Quasimodo in Universal's *The Hunchback of Notre Dame.* This was Chaney's most grotesque portrayal to that time and the makeup required to transform the rugged actor into the monstrous hunchback added 90 pounds to his weight, making his performance all the more remarkable. *The Hunchback* was not filmed as a starring vehicle for Chaney, but his emergence as its star was inevitable, for much of the film's spectacle is devoid of the emotion found in other similar screen stories (such as Griffith's *Orphans of the Storm*) and within such a vacuum, his superb performance stands out sharply. *The Hunchback* has been remade several times but no subsequent version, American or foreign, equals the sweep and power of the original, and to a large extent, this failure rests in the inability of any subsequent Quasimodo to surpass Chaney's portrayal.

Part of Chaney's appeal in his roles rested upon his insistence upon absolute realism where possible, instead of resorting to trickery. For *The Penalty,* in which he played a cripple without legs, Lon had his own legs tightly fastened behind him, giving the highly realistic appearance of one whose limbs had been amputated at the knees. The pain of walking on his knees was evident, and in some scenes he even jumped and landed on them.

Chaney made a series of macabre thrillers at M-G-M with Tod Browning, a past master of the emerging horror genre of the silent era (horror films as we think of them today were mainly of the talkie era) and a director who both appreciated and respected Chaney's artistry. While *The Road to Mandalay, The Unknown, The Blackbird* and *London After Dark* were strong chillers, Chaney's other popular masterpiece, *The Phantom of the Opera,* was made back at Universal. It is another film whose remakes have always fallen short of the original. *The Phantom* was also a hokey film, especially since director Rupert Julian chose to treat his subject less as a mystery and more as a melodramatic cliffhanger, yet the excitement generated by Chaney in the title role and his ability to evoke genuine horror (especially in the famous unmasking sequence) placed this 1925 chiller among the most commercially successful performances of Chaney's career.

When sound arrived, Lon Chaney was uncertain of the future, but a remake of his *The Unholy Three* proved that if anything talkies would further enhance his reputation. It was planned that he would star in *Dracula* (a role that eventually landed in Bela Lugosi's lap and made him a star) but trouble with a growth in his throat had started to give him concern and forced him to enter the hospital, where it was discovered that Lon Chaney had cancer. Ironically, communication became increasingly difficult and he soon found it necessary to resort to the sign language and pantomime he had used as a child; he died soon after.

Picking up the makeup box with which his father had created a career, his son Creighton carried on as Lon Chaney Jr. (later billed simply as Lon Chaney) in horror films of the thirties, but however admirable his efforts, all except *Of Mice and Men* lacked the genuine spark of humanity which had shone through virtually all of his father's portrayals. And so one of the screen's greatest actors, whose talent went far beyond that of personality, was taken at the height of his career, but he left behind a legacy of masterful performances yet to be equaled by subsequent performers. If you've never seen Lon Chaney at work, you've missed a great moment in the history of the movies.

Lon Chaney.

The Miracle Man *brought fame to Chaney and Tom Meighan in 1919, shown here with Betty Compson, Joseph S. Dowling and J. M. Dumont.*

This scene from The Penalty *demonstrates the lengths to which Chaney would go to seek realism. With his legs bound tightly behind him to play the role of the cripple, he took several bone-jarring leaps onto his knees in the course of this 1920 picture.*

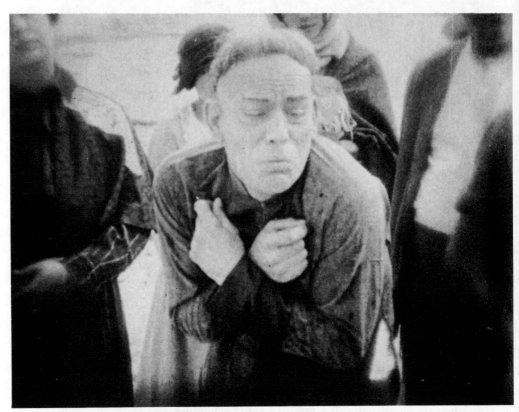

As Yen Sin the laundryman in Shadows, 1922.

The Shock, *1923.*

The Next Corner, 1924, *with Dorothy MacKaill.*

The Hunchback of Notre Dame *in 1923 remains one of Chaney's two* *best-remembered roles.*

The Monster, *1925.*

Tower of Lies, *1925.*

Chaney remade The Unholy Three *(1925) as his debut in talkies in 1930 and appeared to have a bright future ahead when it was discovered that he had cancer.*

Chaney was a master artist with his make-up box. The Road to Mandalay,
1926.

Laugh Clown Laugh, *1928.*

RONALD COLMAN

One of the most debonair and cultured of the silent screen heroes was an impeccable Englishman; a suave, well-mannered gentleman whose charm and grace made him extremely popular in the twenties, and even more so in talkies when audiences could hear him speak. He shared the ability of exuding "quality," regardless of the role in which he was cast, with John Barrymore; yet Ronald Colman appealed to the average man in a way the Great Profile never seemed able to.

Born in England in 1891 to parents of modest means, Colman had to leave school at 16 when his father, a silk importer, died. His first job was that of an office boy for the British Steamship Company where he stayed for five years while rising to the position of junior accountant. A member of the Bancroft Amateur Dramatic Society, he occasionally took part in their plays, but with the advent of World War I young Colman enlisted in the London Scottish Infantry, serving with Lord Kitchener's "Contemptibles," a name given them by the Germans. He saw action in the trenches of France at Ypres, where he broke an ankle escaping from a shell explosion, was hospitalized and released from military service.

A civilian once more, he tried for an appointment in the British Foreign Service, where an uncle was in a position to help, and while awaiting notification of his acceptance, Colman joined George Denby's Pierrot troupe, playing banjo and singing. His first real break came in the person of Lena Ashwell, who offered him a small part as a black-faced servant in *The Maharanee of Arkan.* Greatly pleased with him, Miss Ashwell encouraged Colman, who in turn refused the appointment, which had finally been approved, and concentrated instead on a career in the theatre.

Roles came along in *The Misleading Lady* (with Gladys Cooper) and *Damaged Goods,* and then an offer to make films for George Dewhurst who was then producing at Hepworth. It was during this time that he married stage actress Thelma Raye. General unemployment spread across England during 1920 and theatrical work was difficult to come by; after walking the streets of London in search of a job, Colman decided to try his luck in the United States.

In later years, publicity agents were fond of pointing out that Colman arrived in this country with but $57.00, three clean collars and two letters of introduction, while discreetly overlooking to mention that he had also brought his wife. Months passed without work and Colman's meager sum disappeared before he managed to land a job in *The Dauntless Three,* a play starring the noted Robert Warwick. This was only a walk-on part but it led to roles in *The Night Cap* and *The Silver Fox,* both of which opened with high hopes but closed soon after. Good reviews in both brought him to *The Green Goddess* with George Arliss, and in 1921 the ever-optimistic Colman made a pair of low-budget pictures for Selznick (one with Arliss), neither of which did anything for his career, before landing work with Fay Bainter in a road company doing *East Is West.*

This engagement brought him to Los Angeles, where he tried to find more work in films but without luck; he had to wait until returning to New York City, where he appeared on the stage with Ruth Chatterton in *La Tendresse,* to be discovered and signed by director Henry King. King offered Colman the lead opposite Lillian Gish in *The White Sister* and Colman left immediately for Italy where he filmed the picture that made him a star.

Reviewers and critics, unaware that Colman had previous pictures to his credit, widely praised his "debut" and a second film with Miss Gish followed. It was during the filming of *Romolo* (also in Italy) that Colman and his wife separated quietly and fans were never aware that their new romantic idol was really a married man. While *Romola* gave Colman little chance to advance his career, a handful of interesting roles came his way, including a pair of light comedies with Constance Talmadge, and he was back in harness with *Stella Dallas* in 1925. A series of romantic adventures with Vilma Banky then established him as a permanent fixture on the silent screen.

By this time, fans had come to appreciate the air of tweedy, careless elegance that characterized this darkly dashing leading man. A sense of inherent dignity permeated Colman's screen work, but this was part of the actor's basic personality. He was one of those rare individuals who could truly be called a gentleman—those he knew or worked with had nothing but good words for him—and this quality carried over onto the screen. Colman's polished acting carried him through a succession of hits—*Lady Windermere's Fan, The Dark Angel,*

Kiki, Beau Geste, The Winning of Barbara Worth—and then into talkies.

Sound ruined the careers of many actors, but for Colman it proved an avenue for even greater success. He understood far better than others how to deliver lines at a time when primitive microphones strained to catch them, and in exercising restraint he added considerably to his reputation as a natural actor. Sam Goldwyn chose well when he decided to present Colman to the talkies in the melodramatic role of *Bulldog Drummond* instead of as the romantic idol of his silent films. *Bulldog Drummond* was a success and put Ronald Colman enroute to another two decades of stardom and a belated Academy Award in 1947. His *Lost Horizon, A Tale of Two Cities, The Prisoner of Zenda, Random Harvest* and *The Late George Apley* remain among the classics of the talkie era, and his success with such varied roles is ample testimony to his accomplished skill as an actor.

Colman's marriage to Miss Raye was legally dissolved in 1934, and four years later he married Benita Hume. The two were to enjoy unexpected popularity in the forties with their frequent appearances on Jack Benny's radio show that introduced the fastidious Colman as the comedian's neighbor and brought him roles on several leading radio programs, including his own *The Halls of Ivy* in 1950, a program transferred to television in 1954.

When Ronald Colman passed away from pneumonia in 1958, he was eulogized by many and mourned by all. Known and respected as a man of culture and distinction, he had lived the role in real life. In his long career, Ronald Colman had won virtually all of the honors that any movie star could desire, including a 1955 presentation by the George Eastman House Festival of Fine Arts as one of the five actors of the silent era who had contributed most to the medium of motion pictures. With this tribute, need I say more?

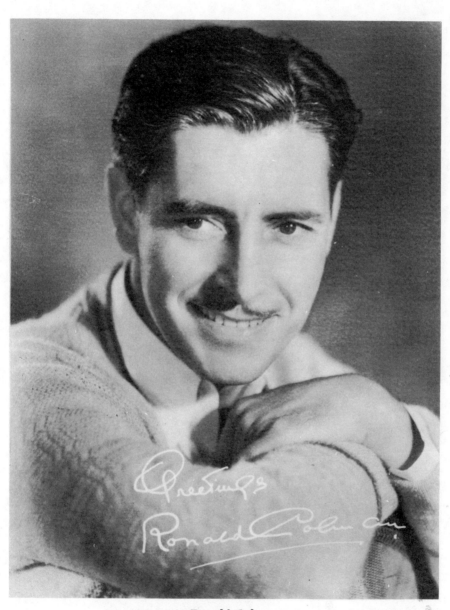

Ronald Colman.

Romola, 1924. *This was Colman's second picture with Lillian Gish but lacked the power of his portrayal in* The White Sister.

Colman and Marie Prevost in Tarnish, *1924.*

The Dark Angel, *1925, one of Colman's romantic affairs with Vilma Banky.*

Belle Bennett as Stella Dallas, *Colman as her husband and Jean Hersholt,*
1925.

With Vilma Banky again in The Night of Love, *1927.*

MAURICE COSTELLO

Maurice Costello set a lot of "firsts" in his rather abbreviated career as a celluloid leading man: he was the first matinee idol, the first to receive fan mail, the first to stand up for the dignity of his profession as actor when other actors were doing menial work between scenes, and the first star to exhibit temperament in an era when actors were considered nothing more than a necessary evil. He was also the first at Vitagraph to receive screen credit under his own name. With all this to his credit, one would have to agree that Costello was an important figure on the early screen, and for a few years he was. Born in Pittsburgh, Maurice had toyed with odd jobs early in life but went on the vaudeville stage in 1894 as a comic. Within a decade, he turned up on Broadway in hits like *Scotland Yard, Kentucky Feud* and *The Cowboy and the Lady,* with stops in legitimate stock and road companies along the way.

Various sources credit his motion picture debut with Edison as early as 1906, but because of the limited availability today of screen subjects of that vintage, and the lack of comprehensive records of the early production companies, it's impossible to verify the exact date now. Nevertheless he did appear at Vitagraph in 1909, where Albert E. Smith engaged him at $30.00 weekly, and it was at Vitagraph that Costello enjoyed his great fame for a few years, winning the first screen popularity contest ever held—a poll of its readers by the *Motion Picture Story Magazine* gave him nearly a half million votes and first place.

His off-screen life—considerably more hectic than the relaxed romantic portrayals he put on film—was largely responsible for the "nervous breakdown" he suffered in 1916–17 that removed him from the screen for over a year. His 1902 marriage lasted until 1927 and gave him two daughters, Helen and Dolores (both worked in his Vitagraph films as youngsters and were to earn greater fame on their own in the twenties), but it almost seemed as if he and his wife were constantly playing musical chairs with each other, as they were alternately separated and reconciled.

But Costello's career was eclipsed mainly because of his age; he was in his late thirties when he came to Vitagraph, already passing his physical prime, and by the time he returned to the screen during World War I, his attractive features had taken on a distinguished look that made him more suited for fatherly roles than for the dashing romanticism of earlier days. More restrained than theatrical in his acting, Costello projected a great deal of sincerity and, convinced that the performance he gave was far more important than the picture in which he played it, he was seen in everything from romantic comedies to a cliffhanging serial.

Character roles became his forte until he retired in 1927. His marital life had continued its stormy course during these years and the marriage of Dolores to John Barrymore temporarily separated him from the family. Costello was quite vehement in his dislike for Barrymore and refused to associate with the family until Jack and Dolores broke up. While he and his wife had both tried to advise the girls on their careers, Costello found his view most often in the minority. He finally shucked the entire responsibility, and obtained a divorce the year he retired. In 1935, he returned to the screen but mainly in extra roles; and when Costello was interviewed in 1941 on the set of *Tin Pan Alley,* he was earning his $12.50 daily and living a modest life, stoutly maintaining that it was much better to be a "has-been" than to be a "never-was."

It's really a shame that motion pictures developed too late in his life to let Maurice stay on top longer; his best remembered role dates back to his portrayal of Sydney Carton in Vitagraph's 1911 *A Tale of Two Cities,* but everyone who ever worked with Costello agreed that no finer actor graced the early screen. He was also known as a gentleman, one whose influence had saved Norma Talmadge's career from ending and one always willing to help others less fortunate than himself. Thanks to this open-checkbook policy with friends and his declining fortunes over the years, the Costello estate at his death was found to be worth a mere $221.55; but he'd enjoyed spending it and his place in screen history had long been secure. After all, who could forget a career with as many firsts to its credit, even if numbered among them was his fate as the first big star to slip from the triumph of fame to the exile of obscurity?

Maurice Costello.

As Sidney Carton in A Tale of Two Cities, *1911.*

The Cambric Mask, *an Alice Joyce feature of 1919.*

Costello with Norma Talmadge in Camille, *1927. Note that his hair was white, a result of his earlier illness.*

RICHARD DIX

With the death of Ernest Carlton Brimmer in 1949 at the age of 54, screen fans mourned the passing of one of the most heroic figures in the motion pictures. As two-fisted Richard Dix, Brimmer had exemplified the clichéd he-man of the movies' golden age, fighting and winning his way over tremendous obstacles in film after film in the twenties. Richard Dix came to the screen rather late in the silent era, but created a hit almost immediately in his career with *The Christian* for Sam Goldwyn, enjoying a mystique that carried him as a top star for over ten years and another decade on the way down.

A large, ruggedly handsome individual whose escapist adventures on celluloid captivated men and women alike, Dix's image was that of the perfect hero, the type born more often in the fertile imagination of a writer's brain than in real life. Western fans took to him quickly, and although he only made seven pictures that could really be classified as horse operas, his appearance in frontier garments as a backwoodsman or pioneer was a natural—he looked as if he had been born to wear buckskins. On the screen, he was seen as a strong, easygoing man on the surface, but hard as steel at his core, the same sort of magic that John Wayne has retained for countless years, and his rugged face carried a hint of the same appeal that Johnny Cash exudes today. With this timeless kind of fascination and the good fortune of strong pictures in which to work, Dix became the personification of an image that was not so widespread as you might think—the strong, determined hero who won by his own noble works, protected the weak and helpless, but remained always ready to move into action when the time came.

Brimmer had attended Northwestern University but left before graduating and went through a variety of odd jobs before deciding to become a stage actor. Finding no work in New York City for inexperienced actors, he changed his name to Richard Dix and managed to join a road company in Pittsburgh. Within a year, he was back on Broadway with sufficient credits behind his name to land him a role supporting William

Faversham in *The Hawk.* Faversham took a liking to the young actor and managed to give him a push in the right direction, from time to time intervening in his favor when a role was at stake.

Dix joined the U.S. Army in 1918, just three months before the Armistice was signed, and after his release from the service turned up in Los Angeles as a member of the Morosco Stock Company. Jeannie McPherson caught his performance, and at her request and insistence Dix submitted to a screen test. Displeased with the results, he didn't bother to pursue the matter further, but Miss McPherson did; and as a result of her influence he was offered a role late in 1920 in a picture called *Not Guilty.* Less than a year later, he was starring in *The Christian* for Goldwyn, a picture that proved to be one of the best roles (and biggest hits) of his career.

From that point on, Richard Dix enjoyed stardom. Seemingly unable to make a flop, he went from one good portrayal to another. As the heroic brother in *The Ten Commandments,* he worked with Rod La-Rocque, whose star was also on the ascent, and by mid-decade, Dix stood forth as one of those few actors whose name alone could attract audiences. And fans were seldom disappointed in what they were offered. His story of the gridiron, *The Quarterback,* is considered one of the most memorable sports pictures of the silent era (and incidentally used several extras from Dartmouth who would become leading box-office personalities in talkie westerns). *Lucky Devil* cast him as a daredevil racing driver and *The Vanishing American* proved to be the most sensitive performance of his career. The story of an Indian cited for heroism in World War I who returned to his western home determined to help his people fight the corrupt political system and its inhumanity towards the Red Man, this film was one of the most realistic social appraisals of the injustice done to the American Indian ever put on the screen. Its effect on the Indian's circumstances was minimal, but for a time, Dix's strong portrayal pricked the conscience of a nation.

When sound arrived, Dix moved over to RKO and continued working, but at a slower pace, turning out only two pictures a year. A heart condition required him to avoid strenuous activity and so the roles became more sedate and fewer in number. No serious complications resulted until 1948, when he suffered a severe attack after completing a series of seven "B" pictures for Columbia based on the exploits of "The Whistler." A few months later Dix's condition began to deteriorate, and he passed on in 1949, still as handsome and determined in appearance as he had been in his heyday two decades before, when his name on the marquee meant money at the box-office.

Best wishes Richard Dix

Richard Dix.

As Brother Paul, Gareth Hughes begs Richard Dix to look after his sister in The Christian, *the 1923 Goldwyn picture that made Dix a star.*

Dix and Bebe Daniels in Sinners in Heaven, *1924.*

Estelle Taylor and Dix in The Ten Commandments, 1923.

Womanhandled, *1926.*

Dix gave a rugged portrayal in Redskin, *1929.*

Dix's role in The Gay Defender *was that of a Mexican bandit redeemed by love. Critics panned this 1927 film but fans ate it up just the same.*

Dix is still remembered for the role of Yancey Cravat in Cimarron, 1930.
*Here he assures the town's "scarlet woman," Estelle Taylor, that she can
count on his support.*

As Sam Houston in Man of Conquest, *a 1939 Republic dramatization of the Texas hero's life. He bears a remarkable resemblance here to a well-known country singer of today.*

DOUGLAS FAIRBANKS

The greatest swashbuckler of them all, he fought pirates, politicians and armies with one hand while winning the fair maiden with the other, sailed the skies on a magic carpet, won France for the Queen and freed England from the grasp of King John—all without even taking a second breath. Errol Flynn may have been a more risqué lover, but he was no more gallant or daring than the Denver-born lad named Douglas Elton Ulman.

Remembered primarily today for all those magical adventures, Ulman enjoyed several careers as Douglas Fairbanks, a breezy and buoyant actor who left a successful stage career in 1915 to join Harry Aitken's Triangle Film Corporation. With *The Lamb,* his first of 43 films, Fairbanks launched a new career that quickly saw him elevated to top stardom throughout the silent era. Doug began in the theatre in 1901 with a role in *Richelieu* at Ford's Theatre (Baltimore) and ended on Broadway in a long-term contract with showman William A. Brady. With the screen drawing so heavily upon the legitimate stage for talent in those early years, it was not surprising that an offer to join Famous Players was tendered in 1913 by David Frohman (for whom Doug made a screen test), but nothing came of these negotiations and Fairbanks remained a fixture on the stage until Harry Aitken managed to sign him two years later.

Doug's salary at Triangle began with $2000 weekly, and in the third and final year was to reach $3000. In addition, his contract called for personal supervision of his pictures by D. W. Griffith, by itself an indication of his stage reputation. Once the story line of Doug's stage hit, *The New Henrietta,* had been adapted to the screen by Griffith for his first picture, Fairbanks was off and running with an ebullient light comedy characterization which he would develop more fully in following Triangle pictures. Doug became the epitome of healthy optimism, breezing his way through adventure after adventure in a light-hearted manner, winning over both story and female lead in a series of satirical contemporary comedies like *His Picture in the Paper, American Aristocracy, Flirting With Fate* and *The Matrimaniac.*

Many of these early Fairbanks vehicles have been revived today, making it possible to study the evolution of the movies' version of "The All-American Boy" long before radio's Jack Armstrong would make the term a household word. Much of Doug's work during his Triangle years was guided by John Emerson and Anita Loos, a very talented director-writer team working under Frank Woods, who found in Fairbanks the perfect medium for their creative expression. A merchant of daydreams, the Fairbanks character took life and his station in it less than seriously, yet forever emerged triumphant despite the fact that his adventures inevitably found him as a man of leisure and wealth—no Horatio Alger stories for this screen hero.

With William S. Hart, Fairbanks reigned supreme as Triangle's top box-office attraction, but he soon tired both of the firm and of his roles. Griffith had not supervised his pictures, as the contract stipulated, and in his second year Doug entertained serious thoughts of leaving Triangle, but friends counseled a more cautious approach—the money was excellent and allowed him time to make more suitable arrangements. Adolph Zukor of Paramount helped Doug to formulate these plans, and in 1917 Fairbanks walked out on his Triangle contract to join Famous Players, where he continued the successful characterization in its Artcraft Pictures. Two years later he participated in the formation of United Artists, with Mary Pickford, Charlie Chaplin and D. W. Griffith as equal partners. There must have been a great sense of achievement in being a partner to the director who had so little use for Doug's acting ability that he had once contemptuously suggested "the jumping jack" hop over to Mack Sennett's Keystone Comedies as a more suitable home for his talent.

By 1920 Doug was thoroughly tired of his "All-American Boy" character, then being successfully parodied by comic Harold Lloyd. His escapist adventures had made Fairbanks one of the screen's leading lights in a mere five years, but Doug decided upon two courses of action, either of which could have cost him his career. He would wed Mary Pickford, "America's Sweetheart," with whom he had fallen in love years before (both had been very recently divorced), and he would begin filming a comic melodrama released as *The Mark of Zorro,* in which he played a dual role as the foppish son of a Spanish grandee who assumed the role of the masked bandit Zorro, to defy a corrupt political regime and bring reform to the people. Fairbanks himself had doubts about Zorro's popularity but audiences flocked to the box-office, banishing all doubts in anyone's mind. Costume swashbucklers were in and so was Doug, who followed with another smash hit in *The Three Musketeers.* Doug's star continued to glow even brighter—his *Robin Hood* and *The Thief of Bagdad* were both elaborate in conception, execution and in earnings, repaying a handsome sum on the million-dollar investments. The public outcry anticipated at his marriage to Pickford had turned out to be further adulation instead, and by 1924 Fairbanks stood at the top of his profession and popularity. Audiences had forgotten the cheerful optimist of the Triangle days and now looked forward to the extravagant costume dramas that marked Doug as the Charlton Heston of his day.

Yet an examination of Fairbanks's work in the twenties clearly reveals that he had only cloaked his earlier character in fancy period dress—there was the same super-athletic Doug exuding the same ebullient optimism of earlier days, but now functioning in a historical atmosphere that reeked of authenticity; for *Robin Hood,* Doug had created a full castle set near the corner of Santa Monica and La Brea in Hollywood which rose 90 feet into the air and helped bring the negative cost to almost $1 million.

Historians and cinema addicts have debated for years whether or not he did his own stunts; athletic as he was, he retained Richard Talmadge on his payroll and Talmadge did double the star occasionally, especially in the later twenties when Doug's timing began to slow. Fairbanks was often (and justly) accused of departing from historical accuracy in his costume pictures, but none ever complained that he passed off poor performances under the disguise of a mask. Fantasy such as he peddled in *The Thief of Bagdad* was the stuff of which dreams are made and no screen personality was more successful in providing the public with what it wanted. Always concerned with production aspects, Fairbanks ran his company with both a firm hand and black humor, but his insistence on innovations—such as the use of Technicolor in *The Black Pirate* (1926) —made Doug's features worth waiting for. Seen today, most of his costume pictures are overly long and too slowly paced to hold the complete attention of modern viewers, but in their time the spectacle and pageantry that took place on the screen were fresh and unequalled, and it was this very element which set Doug's pictures above those of his peers—nobody made historical costume dramas with the same flair.

Doug's health began to fail with the coming of sound and his marriage to Mary Pickford evaporated soon after, but his place on the screen was secure. Certainly the King of the costume epic, none have since come along to take Fairbanks's place, and few have equalled the adulation accorded him by a generation that took this All-American boy into its heart and home as one of its own. His death at 56 came unexpectedly even to friends, few of whom could imagine a world without its King.

Douglas Fairbanks.

Doug with Mary Pickford, Charlie Chaplin and Mary's mother in Omaha, Nebraska, during a World War I bond drive.

With Seena Owen and director Christy Cabanne on the set of his first picture, The Lamb, *1915.*

Doug and Mary, America's King and Queen, at Pickfair shortly after their marriage.

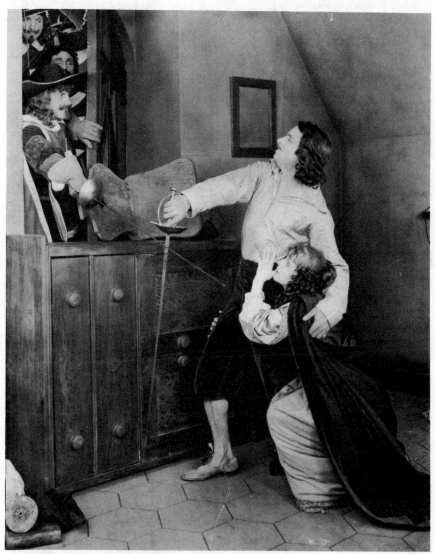

As D'Artagnan in The Three Musketeers, 1921, *Doug protected Marguerite de la Motte from danger.*

With Marguerite de la Motte in The Nut, *1921.*

The Thief of Bagdad, *1924.*

Enid Bennett was Maid Marian to his Robin Hood, 1922.

Don Q, Son of Zorro, *1925*.

Doug drew once more on Alexander Dumas for The Iron Mask *in 1929.*

Doug at his rollicking best in The Black Pirate, *1926.*

The Gaucho, *1928*.

Doug concluded his career on the American screen in 1932 with Mr. Robinson Crusoe. *That's Marie Alba supporting. Two years later, he filmed* The Private Life of Don Juan *in England and then retired.*

WILLIAM FARNUM

William Farnum scored a smashing success in his very first screen role, created a historic sequence that has come to be regarded as one of the most realistic fights ever captured on celluloid, and went on to become one of the biggest stars of his day. Familiar to fans in everything from westerns to the classics, he reigned as the top box-office attraction on the Fox lot during those years when increasing costs and declining receipts took the glamor from Theda Bara. In fact, Bill Farnum's stardom might have easily lasted through the twenties had it not been for an accident and illness that forced him from the screen temporarily early in the decade.

One of three brothers (William, Dustin and Marshall), Bill was born in 1876 to a theatrical family living in Boston, but grew up in Bucksport, Maine, where he received his first taste of the stage when only ten. By the time he arrived on the motion picture screen in 1914, Bill had established a solid stage career with a variety of dramatic roles. Like William S. Hart, who would soon follow him to the screen, Farnum had spent several years touring in *Ben Hur* and would experience worldwide adulation for his rugged he-man roles, a number of which were darn good westerns.

Bill's brother Dustin had also taken to the stage and both made their motion picture debut in epoch-making films of 1914: Bill in *The Spoilers* for Selig and Dustin in *The Squaw Man* for DeMille. Although not a great film, *The Spoilers* was one of the first feature-length pictures that was cinematic in nature. Other feature-length movies had been produced as early as 1912, but most drew heavily on theatrical techniques for staging, resulting in a lack of action and pacing. However, *The Spoilers* (and this was only the first of many translations of Rex Beach's popular novel to the screen) certainly avoided those faults, and in doing so impressed audiences with its realistic approach, part of which came from a real lack of production knowhow on the part of Selig.

While the Selig Polyscope Company was one of the pioneer producers, it was primarily a short picture factory and its initial attempt at a seven-reel story strained the limited creative resources almost to the breaking point. But the story, complete with interwoven subplots, did move right along briskly, and with director Colin Campbell behind the megaphone came off surprisingly well on-screen and at the box-office.

The big moment was the famous fight in which Glennister and McNamara, played by Farnum and Tom Santschi, tried to beat each other to death, pulling no punches and asking no quarter; it seems to be this climactic showdown that has made the Selig version of *The Spoilers* so well remembered. While most screen fights before and after *The Spoilers* were staged (and usually poorly at that), there could be no doubt to those watching in the audiences at the time that Farnum and Santschi were serious. The two men often chuckled in later years while recalling their agreement to a fight to the finish with no hard feelings. After it was completed, both took off a week to recuperate. This most famous of all fistic screen duels was much better staged in subsequent remakes, but the very slickness with which they were done destroyed the realism achieved in 1914.

From the success of *The Spoilers,* which he had not really wanted to make, Bill Farnum went on to Fox and dozens of interesting and popular portrayals—*Les Miserables, The Plunderer, A Tale of Two Cities, The Lone Star Ranger*—which more than justified the $10,000 weekly salary paid him by Fox at a time when a contract year was 52 weeks, not the 40 or less of later decades. For four years, Bill Farnum drew $520,000 a year and enjoyed himself immensely. He bought a seven-acre estate in the Hollywood Hills, two town houses in New York City, and a $450,000 place in Maine, living a life envied by many later stars. His presence at war bond drives during World War I sold some $37 million worth of bonds for the United States, for which he received a belated award some 23 years later. Bill's rapport with critics at the time was almost as good as that he enjoyed with the public and his work in *The Sign of the Cross, Drag Harlan* and *If I Were King* met with continued approval at the box-office and with reviewers.

In the meantime, brother Dustin had reached his peak as a screen star and was fading from the scene, but Bill's career just seemed to steam-roll along. In 1921, a trade journal polled exhibitors to find the most popular personalities and William Farnum was still among the top fifteen. While it's been suggested that Bill's career was slipping when he left the screen in 1922, I personally doubt that one or two poor films could have interrupted his career that much. But his complete absence from the screen, at a time when things were moving so rapidly in new directions, did make it difficult for Bill to reestablish his foothold when he returned, and so in 1925 he reappeared on the stage with roles in *The Buccaneer, Julius Caesar* and *Macbeth,* which kept the husky actor busy for six years.

A comeback attempt in 1931 rested on his deep, resonant voice in talkies, but the 55-year-old actor had to settle for supporting roles. The days of his youth and glory were gone; the Crash of 1929 had cost him over $2 million, and always free with his money when less fortunate actors were in need, he ended his days in genteel poverty, working almost until his death in 1953. He was last seen in *Lone Star,* a 1952 release.

Unlike other early stage actors who had transferred their attention to the screen, Bill's acting was remarkably cinematic in nature and his richly expressive face, with its evident strength and determination, proved much more natural and effective than the flamboyant and theatrical gesturing used by many of his contemporaries. It's sad that so little of his starring work remains, but Fox has recently announced that it will now attempt to preserve the silent films remaining in its vault. Who knows? Perhaps one or more of Bill Farnum's films will turn up as a result.

Farnum's first picture was The Spoilers *for Selig in 1914.*

William Farnum.

Bill with Tom Santchi and Kathlyn Williams in The Spoilers, *tense drama in 1914.*

Farnum and Santchi square off as in the old days, but now it's 1927 and the two were honorary technical directors on the day Gary Cooper and William Boyd re-created the fight scene for Paramount's remake. That's Mary Brian doing the honors between them.

JOHN GILBERT

As writers have recounted the saga of the silent screen, one of the greatest tragedies to unfold was the advent of sound, which wiped out scores of careers almost overnight. No more popular example has been found than the story of John Gilbert. Over the years, it has been fashionable to point to Gilbert as *the* stellar attraction of the silents whose career nosedived into oblivion as a result of the talkies (some have even suggested that his voice was less than masculine) and many cinema fans too young to remember have accepted this fiction as fact. Overnight rags-to-riches-to-rags stories similar to John's have been used by screen writers for decades with success virtually guaranteed (it always comes out a real tear-jerker), yet a closer look at Jack's career, including the types of roles he played best and the changing emphasis which public tastes brought to the screen in the thirties, proves more significant in explaining his failure to remain at the top.

An orphan whose mother had left him behind at birth in Logan, Utah, Jack Gilbert's movie career dated back to Triangle, Tom Ince and 1916 when he appeared as an extra at $2.00 daily in William S. Hart's *Hells Hinges*. At Triangle, he progressed to supporting roles (usually that of the fellow who lost the girl to Charles Ray) and did some work behind the camera in addition to acting; but it was at Fox in the early twenties that Gilbert began to attract a following, and by the time he signed with M-G-M in mid-decade, Jack was well enough known to undertake important roles in big pictures under the guiding genius of Irving Thalberg, who had decided he was star material.

Part of Jack's appeal to the ladies came from his slender moustache, which added just a touch of the daring to his appearance. Without it, Gilbert was just another young actor at Triangle, but once he regrew it after joining Fox, that simple little device added enough distinction to set him apart from the crowd, and except for his role in *The Big Parade*, Gilbert would wear it throughout his career. Although a rather good actor despite the critics' caustic comments about his ability at times,

Jack projected best as a romantic lead but lacked adaptability. But the hotter the romance in the story, the better he came across, and his high-powered performance with Greta Garbo in *Flesh and the Devil* and *A Woman of Affairs* won over even the most cynical female in the audience; for a brief four years, Jack stood at the top of his profession in appeal, billing and as a box-office draw.

Some of Jack's performances weren't really acting; the star had one weakness called vanity, and this most often manifested itself while filming a picture. Quite likely to fall head over heels in love with his leading lady, the resulting on-screen show became more and more realistic as Gilbert pursued a prospective conquest in front of the camera, and by the time his stardom ended, Jack was closing fast behind Valentino as one of the most popular romantic heroes of the screen. During those four years, he had managed to score in hit after hit with such a monotonous regularity—*The Merry Widow, He Who Gets Slapped, La Boheme, The Big Parade, Man, Woman and Sin, The Cossacks* and his roles with Garbo—it almost seemed as though the applause would never stop. But stop it did, and when it happened Gilbert was shaken to the core. The advent of sound combined with the Great Depression and a new public mood to destroy the market for the extravagant romantic pictures in which he had worked best, and Jack was lost.

Other roles came his way, but Gilbert didn't seem at home as a hoodlum or tough guy, and while he tried desperately to make the change of gears, the necessary drive seemed to disappear. His cocky attitude of stardom disappeared, replaced by an uncertainty, confusion and then depression—natural enough when you pull the rug out from under a high flier. Jack's first pictures with sound had not helped him make the transition easily; *Redemption* was reworked time and again until the salvage job was really unsalvageable, and *His Glorious Night* became unintentionally humorous when Jack made love to Renee Adoree for the first time with words.

Jack's press made matters even worse by getting under his skin with ease. Although the great lover's voice was not any worse than several other actors who were to succeed in talkies (he even took voice lessons to improve it), there were those who seemed convinced that one had to be "different" to be a great lover on the screen and that Jack's voice placed him in that category. The sly insinuations got back to Gilbert, whose manhood had already been shaken considerably by the change of direction in his career; in a sense, Valentino was fortunate. Had he lived, his career would undoubtedly have faced an equally rugged transition and one that might have wiped out the legend overnight.

Gilbert's personality changed within a year from that of a light-hearted happy individual to one bitter and morose with failure, who no longer enthusiastically greeted his many friends with a hail of words; it was almost as though he feared to talk. In 1932, Garbo (who had made the leap from silents to sound with skillful timing) insisted on Jack as her leading man in *Queen Christina,* and for a brief time he became the old John Gilbert that all Hollywood had known and loved; but the fire didn't last long. Garbo was no longer interested in him, and although the picture was a success, it did nothing for his career. After a minor role in *The Captain Hates the Sea,* he retired to seclusion and drink. Old friends found him intolerable and soon he was left alone, which only intensified his bitterness and reinforced the feeling that he had been betrayed and sacrificed. Gilbert was found dead by his valet in January 1936. He was 38.

Alcohol was the culprit, but those who knew and loved Jack Gilbert were aware that his broken spirit had nothing left to live for. It had been a long, hard but glorious path that he had traveled, from unwanted orphan to near-legend, but the abrupt end was most tragic; a young man, Jack Gilbert remained a holdover from an era that died very suddenly and without his even realizing that it was gone. The last few years must have been a great puzzle to the star, unable to figure what had gone wrong—and even worse, unable to stem the tide of failure.

As Jack's best films were made for Fox and M-G-M, very little has been seen of his work for years, but hard pressed for cash these days, M-G-M has reached back into its vault and retrieved *The Big Parade* and other classics of a bygone era for renovation, restoration and reissue, probably on television. When this day comes, don't miss this performance; it would please Jack wherever he is to know that a new generation is watching.

John Gilbert.

Golden Rule Kate, *1917.*

With Aileen Pringle in His Hour, *1924, one of Elinor Glyn's all-consuming romances.*

Starting as an extra in 1916, Gilbert's career rose slowly but he began to attract notice at Fox in the early twenties with vehicles like Cameo Kirby *in 1923. His companion—Alan Hale.*

John's early roles were mainly period pieces, as in Bardeleys the Magnificent, 1926.

Sparks flashed on-screen as Gilbert and Garbo came together in Flesh and the Devil, 1927.

A happy and relaxed John Gilbert at home. Only a few years later, he would close his door to the world and in despair and anger, drink himself to death.

These two scenes from A Woman of Affairs *represent the end of John Gilbert's devil-may-care attitude toward life. A year later in 1930, he would secretly cry at his image on the screen and wonder exactly what had gone wrong.*

Garbo and Gilbert enjoyed an on-off flirtation-infatuation that Gilbert took as Love, *1927.*

Garbo demanded Gilbert as her leading man in Queen Christina *and John regained his old spirits briefly in 1933. But Garbo made it quite clear that there was nothing left between them and the film unfortunately did not rejuvenate his ailing career.*

SESSUE HAYAKAWA

With the deep feelings against certain minorities, and especially Orientals, in this country during the early part of the century, the popularity of Kintaro Hayakawa stands out as a distinct paradox. A native of Chiba, Japan, Hayakawa had been destined for a military career when a punctured eardrum brought that possibility to a quick end. By the time he was in his mid-thirties, the slender Japanese had become successful beyond his fondest dreams; he was known to millions of moviegoers as actor Sessue Hayakawa. For this millionaire who produced his own pictures with fantastic success, it had all come about in a most unusual fashion.

Once the door closed on his military career, Hayakawa had enrolled at the University of Chicago and arrived in this country in 1911 to study political science. During a vacation in Los Angeles two years later, he organized a group of young actors and presented a political melodrama to local audiences. Thomas H. Ince was sitting in the front row when *The Typhoon* opened, and as the curtain rang down the movie producer hurried backstage and invited the fledgling actor and his group to perform for the movie camera. Ince recognized that their story would make a strong screenplay—a man who deliberately confessed to a murder committed by a diplomat to give the murderer sufficient time to complete a vital mission—self-sacrifice of the highest order.

Amused but not terribly interested in the proposal, Hayakawa attempted to hasten Ince's departure by agreeing to do it but at a salary of $500 weekly. To his surprise, Ince readily agreed and Hayakawa found himself with a six-month contract. As Ince had predicted, *The Typhoon* made a powerful film and Sessue was on his way. When the contract with Ince ended, Hayakawa moved over to Paramount, where his salary would eventually reach $6000 weekly, and almost immediately repeated his success opposite Fannie Ward in *The Cheat,* a compelling drama of a woman who borrowed money to help her husband and then tried to renege on her bargain when she was unable to make the payment.

From 1915 through 1918, Sessue Hayakawa starred in a lengthy series for Paramount (many of which also featured Jack Holt), rising to a stature enjoyed by no other non-Caucasian actor on the screen. Varying heroic roles with villainous portrayals, Sessue's strong sense of dramatics and relaxed acting style proved a popular combination at the box-office. His popularity was so great that Paramount cast him opposite most of its well-known leading ladies without criticism and supporting actors who worked with Hayakawa found that their careers were helped.

Sessue lived the part of star both on and off the screen. He owned a greystone castle at the corner of Franklin and Argyle in Hollywood (since replaced by a motel), where lavish entertainment in the early twenties was almost continuous—weekly luncheons were held for 150, buffet suppers for 900 with three different orchestras playing, and sit-down dinners hosted for 250 guests. Seven servants ran the place while Sessue and his wife, Tsuru Aoki (also a screen star) worked hard and played hard. Charles Ray with his solid gold doorknobs had nothing on the most cunning Oriental of the screen—Hayakawa owned a gold-plated Pierce-Arrow complete with liveried footman, but only until Roscoe Arbuckle managed to acquire a duplicate; when the original was no longer one of a kind, Sessue donated his car to the Long Island Fire Department.

Organizing his own company (Haworth) in 1919, Sessue hired former Keystone general manager George W. Stout to operate the studio, which was located on the corner of Sunset and Hollywood Boulevard. Hayakawa spent a total of $350,000 to make each picture, $200,000 of which he drew in salary as the star. As Haworth turned out 25 pictures in a little more than three years, it's obvious that Sessue was popular, lived well and worked hard. His choice of roles was out of the ordinary and ranged from romantic tragedy through fantasy. Even racial discrimination was worked into some of the stories.

Sessue's fans responded with enthusiasm, and until the mid-twenties, Hayakawa continued to deliver consistently strong performances in powerful dramas like *The Tong Man* (a fine print of this is available for those interested in watching a real actor of the silent era at work). But by 1924, his pictures began to show a decline at the boxoffice and Sessue left American pictures for England, where he starred in *Sen Yen's Devotion*. Next he toured Europe. Three years later, the actor donated his Hollywood castle to a religious organization and moved back to the New York stage. Sessue lost most of his holdings in the Crash of 1929, but made only one more film in Hollywood. In all his years in the United States, Hayakawa had never spoken English without a heavy accent, in contrast to his wife, who conversed fluently in precise English, and there was little work for him in the early talkies. Moving back to the Orient, he starred for four years in Japanese movies.

But the rise of Japanese militarism convinced Hayakawa to leave before it was too late and he next appeared in France, where he made 17 additional features and sat out World War II. Although he had been cast in three postwar American pictures before signing for the role of the Japanese commandant of a wartime jungle prison camp in Siam in the David Lean-Sam Spiegel production of *The Bridge on the River Kwai*, Hollywood was taken by surprise when his fine performance was screened. Once the word went out that Hayakawa was a distinguished actor and star from the past, he was suddenly in demand again. Sessue has chosen his roles carefully since and is only occasionally seen today, but when he does work, it's a masterful performance by one who understands the art of acting.

With Fannie Ward in The Cheat, *a Cecil B. DeMille production of 1915 that established Hayakawa as a star who would be around a long time.*

Sessue Hayakawa at the height of his screen fame. The auto is a gold-plated Pierce-Arrow which the star gave away when Roscoe Arbuckle acquired one like it.

Alien Souls. *That's Sessue's wife Tsuru Aoki at the right.*

Sessue's dramatic acting was intense, but at the same time did not rely upon overly emphasized gestures or exaggerated pantomime.

Cast opposite many of Paramount's top female attractions, Hayakawa played both hero and villain with ease. This scene is from The Secret Game *with Myrtle Stedman in 1918.*

Myrtle Stedman again, as Sessue contemplates her past, present and future in his own inscrutable oriental manner.

Hayakawa roared back into the public eye with his 1958 portrayal of a Japanese prison camp commandant in The Bridge on the River Kwai.

*These two scenes from one of Sessue's pictures in the early twenties pro-
vide an inside look at the magic of the movies. The first is as the audience
saw it on the screen; the second shows the set on which it was filmed.
What was that about the romance of the movies?*

The Tong Man, *1920, with Helen Jerome Eddy.*

JOHNNY HINES

Sophisticated light comedy was all the rage during the twenties and almost every screen actor tried his hand at it once or twice. A few even made it their specialty and became great popular favorites. Slapstick comedy was easy enough for those whose appetite could take pies and pratfalls as they came along, but walking the high wire between comedy and drama required a much finer touch and one that is almost indefinable, especially when relying upon the art of pantomime alone. Once dialogue entered the picture, it was easy enough to understand the success of actors like William Powell in light comedies of the thirties, but look over Bill's career to that point and you'll find little indication of this talent in his previous work.

When sophisticated comedy of the twenties is mentioned, three practitioners of the art come to mind without hesitation—Reginald Denny, William Haines and Johnny Hines. All three were very popular with fans and enjoyed the blessings of stardom for about a decade. While Denny, with his Doug Fairbanks style of comedy mixed with adventure, was probably the most popular of the trio, my personal vote goes to Johnny Hines without question. That cocky kid with the ever-laughing eyes made one mistake right after another, but somehow he always managed to come out ahead, just as you knew he would.

A Golden, Colorado, boy educated at the University of Pittsburgh and City College of New York, Johnny's stage debut began almost at the very top—working with William Gillette in *Sherlock Holmes* and then George M. Cohan in *The Little Millionaire.* In the process, he earned quite a reputation on the stage as an eccentric dancer and comic before joining William A. Brady's World Films in 1914 with a part in a Robert Warwick feature, *The Man of the Hour.* Johnny added zest to *Tillie Wakes Up,* Marie Dressler's sequel to her 1914 Keystone *Tillie's Punctured Romance,* and did fine roles in *Alias Jimmy Valentine* and other World pictures. Drama occupied much of his five years with World, with only occasional forays into comedy, but Johnny's real fame was still to come in a very long series of two-reel comedies for C. C. Burr's Master Films beginning in 1920. He was cast as Torchy, a juvenile who got in and out of trouble faster than the director could dream it up. Distributed by the newly formed Educational exchanges of Earle Hammons, one of the largest comedy distributors of the twenties, The Torchy Comedies reached a much wider audience than the ordinary independent series of that time and caught on strongly with exhibitors.

Johnny moved into full-length features in the twenties, first for C. C. Burr and then First National. Virtually all of his work from the Torchy Comedies on was directed by his brother Charles, who had given up a long career in musical comedy, stock and vaudeville to apply his light-hearted touch to Johnny's career. Charles Hines had a knack of bringing out the best in his brother and the two enjoyed more than a decade of uninterrupted success as a team.

The basic Johnny Hines was easy enough for audiences to identify with. A variation on the red-blooded All-American boy made popular at Triangle years before by Doug Fairbanks, Johnny usually started off on top of the situation, which made his brash, almost cocky attitude believable—here was a fellow who knew his way around. The jaunty straw hat and immaculate white spats added to the picture of confidence, and no matter how bad things became, Johnny never once showed real despair. *Burn 'Em Up Barnes, The Crackerjack, Conductor 1492*—the hits rolled along one after another, and filled with action, adventure and a healthy dose of romance, they appealed to the entire family.

Coming about midway in his career, *The Speed Spook* (1924) fitted the Hines formula perfectly. As a successful auto racer, Johnny returned to his home town after a big race. Everyone was on hand to greet the image of success—the small town boy who had made good. Enter his childhood flame, now grown up and helping her father operate an auto dealership that wasn't doing very well. In fact, the cars were slowly ruining the agency's reputation, as none of the small number sold seemed dependable and the bad reputation spread fast in the small town. Smelling a rat, Johnny took an active hand in restoring the agency's good will by offering to race one of the cars, and from this point on it was one mishap after another as the scheming old codger out to ruin the girl's father did his best to stop the ever-smiling hero. Sounds like an up-to-date attempt to run the rancher off his property to buy it cheap, doesn't it? The seven reels moved along at a brisk pace with Hines winning out in the end, but not until considerable doubt had passed through the audiences' minds.

One of the greatest virtues of Johnny's early features was his novel, often ingenious, approach to tight situations that brought forth streams of laughter, but as the twenties wore on his work began to take on a sameness, especially after he moved from the independent productions of Burr to First National release. Reviewers complained that Johnny only changed the settings and that his scripts were too vague in story line— it was a successful formula that seemed to be wearing out its welcome, for situations and production values embellished the First National releases, but with no concurrent attention to strengthening the plot. But despite his critics and detractors, Johnny Hines just kept turning out good family pictures and families continued turning out to see them.

There's no doubt today that Hines's best remembered pictures came from the years he spent with Burr. Spreading from ear to ear on the screen, his million-dollar smile was bound to win over audiences, and with clever material and an engaging personality, Johnny had a winning combination for much of his career. Sound removed Johnny from the starring ranks but failed to keep him out of the business. The comedy that he had been doing for a decade was still popular, and after leaving the screen he slipped his sharp wit comfortably into an easy chair as a writer, turning out choice bits for well-known short subjects like the "Pete Smith Specialties" in the forties. Death took Johnny Hines in 1970, but those who knew him are convinced that with Johnny's firm belief that you can't keep a good man down, he is still performing somewhere; and in a sense they're correct. Occasionally he can be seen cavorting across the screen at John Hampton's Silent Movie Theatre in Los Angeles, looking every bit as confident and cheerful as he did in 1924.

A scene from the third of the Torchy Comedies, 1920.

Johnny wraps up another one in The Speed Spook, *1924.*

Burn 'em Up Barnes, *1921.*

Johnny's romantic touch was seldom appreciated by mother.

Johnny and Louise Lorraine in The Wright Idea.

Comedy like this made Hines's pictures delightful family entertainment.

JACK HOLT

Few silent stars consistently brought as much adventure to the screen as one Charles John Holt, but then few came to motion pictures with as colorful a background as this lad, who had been requested to leave his studies at Virginia Military Institute during his third year. To say that Jack Holt was a fun-loving hell-raiser might be a bit strong, but he certainly let no grass grow under his feet. While his parents' desire that their son become an Army officer could no longer be accomplished the gentlemanly way, Jack was on his own but his engineering studies came in handy. His first job after leaving VMI was that of a sandhog, working on the Hoboken tunnel. Leaving this behind, he wandered westward, stopping in Alaska where mining, fur trading and other odd jobs caught his fancy for four years.

When Jack returned, he settled briefly in Oregon, working on a ranch long enough to learn cowpunching and riding, then moving southward again. Landing in San Francisco broke and without a prospect in sight in 1913, Holt learned that a movie director shooting on location nearby was in need of someone willing to take a thirty-foot fall and he hurried over to investigate. The ten minutes of work was far more profitable than any gold strike he had made in Alaska, and although it broke two of his ribs, Jack had a stake. He had also caught the eye of director William Nigh, who offered to use him on a regular basis. When the crew returned to Los Angeles, Holt accompanied it south.

Cast first in villainous roles, Jack Holt quickly became a busy actor and a familiar sight to early fans of the screen. Like so many of the movies' character actors, few in the audience knew his name; but when Jack appeared on the screen, all realized what he was up to, and it was seldom good news for the heroine. Holt's screen reformation and the real beginning of his career came while working with the serial team of Grace Cunard and Francis Ford, who cast him on the side of the law. A prominent part in *Liberty, A Daughter of the USA* in 1916 found Jack wearing the uniform of a U.S. Army officer—in a sense he had fulfilled his family's wish.

A popular actor in society dramas (especially those of Sessue Hayakawa) during the World War I years, Jack found his true metier as a son of the West in the early twenties and went on to become one of the best-loved, yet not really significant western heroes of the twenties. His tall, lean form was capped by a long, angular face and a jutting jaw permanently punctuated by a dapper moustache. The ever-present squint of steel blue eyes seemed to signify that he meant business and those foolish enough to lock horns with our hero soon learned that Jack Holt never fooled around. Although he was as much at home in evening dress as in a saddle, fans preferred the rough, tough Holt and Jack spent much of the decade playing soldier of fortune, military officer or western hero.

When sound arrived late in the decade, Holt's deep and brusque voice added to his he-man image; Jack had little trouble finding work in the plethora of westerns and crime melodramas of the thirties. Although Jack Holt never broke out of the B hero mold, he proved one of the best. Occasionally, one of his early talkies appears on a tv late show and reaffirms just how much less complex the world really was only three decades ago.

Jack enlisted in the U.S. Army in 1942, rising to the rank of major, and in a sense this was fitting. After all, he had played a military officer so often that it must have been second nature to him. The war ended his starring career and after discharge from the service, he returned to supporting roles. His death in 1951 closed the book on a long and successful career that had brought him fans the world over; no one could play Jack Holt as well as Jack.

Jack Holt.

Jack with Grace Cunard, who was responsible for casting him in heroic parts.

Jack (r) played villains in his early screen appearances in Cleo Madison's pictures.

Jack's family had wanted him to become an Army officer. He obliged them many times in his long career, as in this scene from The Secret Game, *1918.*

. . . fans liked him best in outdoor epics like The Call of the North, *1921. You can believe that Francis MacDonald is taking the warning seriously.*

While Jack was at home in drawing room drama like After the Show *with Lila Lee in 1924 . . .*

The grim look of determination in Man Unconquerable *is fair warning that Holt's about to get rough in this 1922 drama.*

Jack Holt was a natural for the horse operas like Avalanche, *1928. Toward the close of the silent era, he found great popularity with western fans.*

Jack continued in he-man roles well into the thirties, loving and leaving ladies like Jean Arthur . . .

Jack with his daughter Jennifer and son Charles Jr. in 1947. The younger Holt was well-known as Tim Holt, RKO western star who had received excellent reviews for his non-western performances.

. . . but this pose from The Border Legion *in 1930 is how Holt's fans prefer to remember him.*

HOUDINI

In the days before sophisticated production techniques and trick camera
work became routine, the silent movies presented some real-life heroes
on the screen. Perhaps the greatest of these was Erich Weiss, who came
along just as the movies' primitive days were ending; and in that transi-
tional period between 1918–23, no stage name evoked more fascination
than that of Mr. Weiss's pseudonym, Harry Houdini. An accomplished
escape artist, lecturer and showman extraordinaire, Houdini had left his
position as a lining cutter in a clothes factory for the bright lights of
show business, and in doing so captivated a nation whose well-known
gullibility preceded P. T. Barnum's astute observations by several decades.
Houdini's entry into movies was almost preordained; he had conquered
all other entertainment media and what better showcase than film was
then available for a mass audience to see his accomplishments?

Houdini's interest in the motion picture was fed by the vast inroads
it had made in vaudeville audiences and when B. A. Rolfe offered to
star the escape artist in a serial, he accepted without hesitation. Once his
1918 theatrical tour was over, Houdini arrived in New York City, and
with Arthur B. Reeve (a popular writer of fiction who had previously
created some interesting serials) he began constructing a suitable script.
The result was *The Master Mystery* (1919) with Houdini playing
Quentin Locke, the secret service agent whose mission was to thwart the
Automaton, one of the most unlikely villains in cliffhanger history. This
mechanical monster seemed to have a human brain of its own, and sure
enough the final chapter revealed it to be nothing more than an ordinary
villain in a steel suit. But in the 14 intervening episodes, Houdini had
an opportunity to display a wide variety of his best tricks, from freeing
himself as he dangled precariously above a pot of boiling acid to matching
wits with a set of locks as a heavy freight elevator hurled down on his
exposed form. It was deep melodrama, but good clean fun, and Houdini
eventually earned several thousand dollars after suing Rolfe for his share.

But Jesse Lasky felt that Houdini had more box-office potential than the serial had indicated and signed him for two Artcraft specials. Produced early in 1919 in California, *The Grim Game* was written by Reeve and John W. Gray to give Houdini ample opportunities to display his seemingly miraculous abilities, including a wing-to-wing transfer between two planes while in mid-air. This escapade would have been duck soup for Harry, except for a fractured left wrist he had received earlier in filming. Thus a double performed the actual stunt, which turned out just a bit differently than the script had called for. Locking wings by mistake, the two planes fell to earth, disengaging just before the crash. Director Irving Willat caught it all on film and rewrote the script to include the spectacular scene; clever editing intercut closeups of Houdini and made it appear that the star had actually performed and survived the stunt.

Despite the ballyhoo that revolved around this scene, *The Grim Game* only grossed about $200,000 in world release, or about half of what it should have earned, but that autumn Harry began to work on *Terror Island,* the second of the two-picture pact. Filmed at Catalina with fast-moving, fantastic stunts and spectacular escapes, this one grossed even less than *The Grim Game,* for the word had spread—Harry was no actor. His histrionic range was limited to two expressions—one of great surprise and the other a brow-wrinkling, emotionless state of deep thinking.

A short man whose muscular build made him appear to be a bit on the stocky side, Houdini's romantic scenes (a necessity at the time) proved quite wooden and lifeless. What long-limbed beauty could go mad over a runt who walked around with a near-permanent scowl on his face? About the only time Harry appeared to be at home on the screen was while he was effecting an escape, but these sequences were also slightly unbelievable to audiences, although they were filmed without intercutting for the most part, a technique that should have convinced even the most confirmed skeptic that Harry Houdini was really no fake. Taking the box-office message, Paramount failed to renew the contract and so Houdini left for a six-month tour of Great Britain. The huge crowds that greeted his arrival along the way convinced the usually perceptive escape artist that his movies had been responsible and his flagging enthusiasm was renewed.

Returning to the United States, Harry purchased a Hoboken processing laboratory and established the Houdini Picture Corporation to film his own script, *The Man From Beyond.* This story of a man brought to life after spending a frozen century in an ice block in the Yukon, then searching for his former lady friend (discovered to be the great-grand-daughter of the woman he had once loved), was not a bad one, but

Houdini removed any semblance of reality by the hero's matter-of-fact acceptance of a changed world. Indeed, without seeing the first reel today, the remainder of the film has little motivation because of this. The one redeeming aspect of *The Man From Beyond* rested in his rescue of the girl from a canoe about to go over Niagara Falls, but once again, few in the audiences believed that the sequence was real, even though Harry had risked his life in filming it. Personal appearances with each major opening helped the picture's receipts considerably and with his faith in himself vindicated, Houdini turned to filming *Haldane of the Secret Service,* which he turned over to FBO for release. Disgruntled with the publicity campaign that FBO concocted for the picture's release, Houdini ended up financing a major advertising effort of his own to help the picture and barely broke even. He disbanded his company and brought his screen career to a close.

Five pictures in five years and it was all over. On October 6, 1926, Houdini died in a Detroit hospital of peritonitis following a ruptured appendix. The world's greatest mystifier had also conquered motion pictures in a sense, but not in quite the fashion he had set out to. Houdini's personality on the stage sparked an enthusiasm in live audiences that his screen image failed to ignite, leaving only his masterful stunts and escapes to retain interest, and as few believed them real anyway, this was not enough. Had Houdini entered films in 1913, it is quite likely that he could have succeeded wildly—Pearl White did, and her acting was far from fantastic. But there was a change in the composition of movie audiences that began taking place as Harry moved to the screen and this, combined with his inability to loosen up and appear natural on-screen, accounted in large part for his failure to master the medium of movies completely.

But Harry Houdini was and is a legend and remaining prints of his pictures are fascinating, for without this celluloid image, America's greatest escape artist and debunker of spiritualism would be nothing more than another lifeless figure in books such as this. It's seldom that you have the opportunity to watch a legend in action, but with Houdini, it's possible to backtrack through time to a distant day when Erich Weiss was in his prime and he alone was in a position to save humanity from the evil Automaton—it's still great fun.

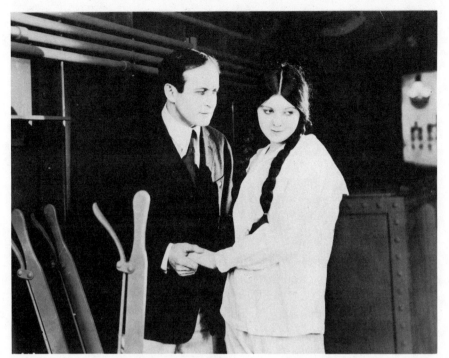

Harry Houdini with Lila Lee in a lighter moment from Terror Island, 1920.

These fellows couldn't be serious! If chains and straight jackets, trunks and locks couldn't stop the famed escape artist, what makes them think a few mortal hands can do it? From Terror Island.

ROD LAROCQUE

Ah, Rod LaRocque—what a name, and what memories it conjures up! Over the years, Rod has become something of a symbol of the Hollywood glamor that has long since disappeared from the former movie capital, and the fact that he married Vilma Banky in 1927 only adds to the aura of mystery and romance that surrounded him. Yet Rod's career is a fine example to use when playing the "What's in a name?" game. The son of a Chicago hotelman, LaRocque's acting career had started in 1905 at the age of seven and for the remainder of his youth, playing child and juvenile roles on the stage and in touring companies alternated with occasional periods of schooling.

Rod eventually joined Essanay, where he worked in many of Bryant Washburn's pictures, and when Essanay collapsed, he left Chicago for New York City to resume his stage career. LaRocque had the misfortune of appearing in two consecutive ill-fated plays produced by showman William A. Brady before he landed a role in Billie Burke's 1918 Paramount picture, *Let's Get a Divorce*. The strength of this role led to a contract with Goldwyn, and Rod appeared in five more pictures; but notice seemed to escape the slender 6′ 3″ actor, and despite roles in a wide variety of film fare, LaRocque periodically found it necessary to return to the stage to keep busy. But Rod's rise began under the guiding hand of Cecil B. DeMille with the role of the rich and negligent contractor whose greed destroyed his mother, friends and himself in the modern segment of *The Ten Commandments*.

Putting the young actor under contract, DeMille featured Rod in *Triumph* and then in *Feet of Clay*, giving him more to do in each film. DeMille enjoyed making stars out of unknowns; before they became public figures, he could work them inexpensively and then let them go for others to use once their salary demands began to rise—it was a "no-star"–small-expense policy of production that gave the putteed director his reputation as a star maker.

Ernst Lubitsch borrowed Rod for the role of the Captain of the Guard in *Forbidden Paradise,* a risqué satire about a queen (played by Pola Negri, who naturally starred), whose amorous adventures helped her to forget the many tribulations of her position, and the film's great success with critics and at the box-office brought LaRocque closer to the top. A role as Lillian Rich's bankrupt husband in *The Golden Bed* for DeMille followed and in the fall of 1925, Rod finally received star billing in *The Coming of Amos.* For the next few years, it was one romantic adventure after another for the new star, who had spent more than a decade in search of the actor's golden reward, and with roles in *Braveheart, Gigolo, Resurrection, The Fighting Eagle, Stand and Deliver* and *Captain Swagger,* Rod LaRocque became one of the more popular of the replicas turned out of Hollywood's romantic hero mold.

His fame never quite came up to that of Ramon Novarro or John Gilbert; indeed, LaRocque stood almost shoulder-to-shoulder with Ricardo Cortez in the late twenties, but Rod's marriage to Miss Banky in 1927 was a coup many American men dreamed of and remains as one of Shadowland's most spectacular ceremonies, and certainly one of the top social events of any season. As Miss Banky was Hungarian, the two could hardly communicate at the time, but their desire to have a simple wedding went unheeded by Sam Goldwyn (for whom the bride worked) and Sam "produced" the wedding, a magnificent affair at the Church of the Good Shepherd in Hollywood. Although he was suing Rod at the time, Cecil B. DeMille was best man, Sam Goldwyn gave the bride away and Tom Mix arrived driving a four-horse coach to whisk the newlyweds away to their reception at the Beverly Hills Hotel. Goldwyn's detractors rumored that the food was mostly papier-mâché and for display only, but the producer had really spared nothing in outdoing all previous (and most future) Hollywood weddings.

Their decision to tie the knot also seemed to mark the beginning of the end for both Rod and Vilma. Only a small handful of pictures came their way before sound took over the destinies of Hollywood's elite and Miss Banky, who spoke very little English, was almost finished by the technical innovation. A year spent with a vocal coach and voice lessons amounted to little, and when she left the American screen to make pictures in Europe, Vilma was accompanied by her husband. The two made a few films together and vacationed before returning to Hollywood, where LaRocque gradually drifted into the real estate business. With his many friends in the movie colony, Rod became quite prosperous over the years by helping the elite of the screen engage in the game of musical house that remained a part of the ritual in which all rising (and falling) movie stars participated.

Although his fame was brief and founded on no particular role or spectacular acting performance, Rod LaRocque's name was so well linked with the era in which he worked that when Paramount filmed *Sunset Boulevard* in 1950, Rod was asked for permission to use both his and Miss Banky's name in a line of dialogue that has since become priceless. In a scene recalling the departed glamor of Hollywood's most fascinating era, William Holden looked out at Gloria Swanson's swimming pool and casually remarked, "Vilma Banky and Rod LaRocque must have swum in that pool a thousand nights ago." In reality, Miss Banky was never able to swim a stroke. To the public, Rod became just another casualty of sound and except for periodic mention of his name in connection with the departed glamor of the silent screen, LaRocque and Vilma Banky lived a quiet, devoted life together until his death in 1967. Rod never looked back with regret and actually seemed to enjoy life more after leaving the screen than when he was pursued by visions of panting females, all of whom would have gladly traded their humdrum existence for one night with Rod LaRocque!

Rod with Betty Burbridge and Edward Arnold in an early Essanay picture.

Rod and Mabel Normand in Goldwyn's A Perfect 36, *1918.*

His role in The Ten Commandments *with Leatrice Joy in 1923 marked the beginning of LaRocque's rise to real screen fame.*

Feet of Clay, 1924, with Vera Reynolds.

Rod with Arthur Hoyt in The Coming of Amos, *1925.*

Rod, Lillian Rich and Theodore Kosloff in The Golden Bed, *1925.*

A change of pace in Red Dice, *1926. Down and out when the picture opened, LaRocque sold himself for one year of high living. At the end of that time, he was to be killed for a large insurance policy taken on his life.*

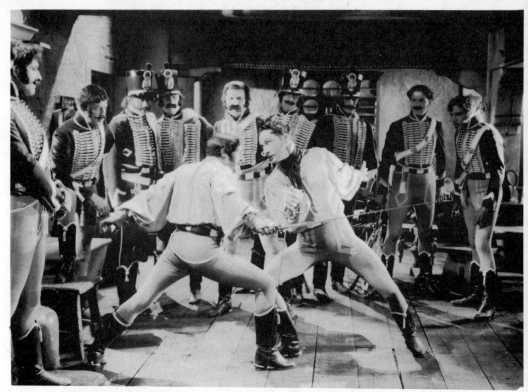

Rod as The Fighting Eagle, *a 1927 swashbuckling adaptation of Sir Conan Doyle's "The Adventures of Gerard."*

Resurrection, *with Delores Del Rio in 1927.*

Beau Bandit *for RKO in 1930 was among Rod's few talkies and final
screen roles.*

ELMO LINCOLN

Had Edgar Rice Burroughs never created a fictional ape-man named Tarzan, Elmo Lincoln's screen career might well have been an even more brief and insignificant episode in movie history. But Burroughs did invent the character in 1912 for the October issue of *All-Star Magazine* and some five years later an obscure actor named Otto Lincolnhelt rose overnight to stardom as the "Lord of the Jungle."

Lincoln had arrived in California after bumming his way around the country for months and found work as an extra in several of D. W. Griffith's short films, beginning with *The Battle of Elderbush Gulch* in 1913. He appeared on-screen in minor roles in *The Birth of a Nation*, but the barrel-chested would-be actor's most notable role was that of "The Mighty Man of Valor" who defended Belshazzar against the troops of Cyrus with tremendous strokes of his sword in the Babylonian episode of *Intolerance*. Beyond these few credits, little was known of Elmo until he was cast as Tarzan by Bill Parsons, whose National Film Corporation had bought screen rights from Burroughs in 1917.

A variety of stories abound concerning Elmo's signing for the role, but no male lead had been secured at the time Parsons's crew left for Louisiana in late August 1917. Director Scott Sidney stopped in New Iberia, but found Morgan City more to his liking and it was there that the original Tarzan appeared. Once location scenes had been secured, the crew returned to Los Angeles in October and the remainder of the eight-reel feature was shot at the E. & R. Jungle Film Company's studio, on a yacht off San Pedro, in Griffith Park and Topanga Canyon. Publicity for the New York premiere stated that *Tarzan of the Apes* had been "produced in the wildest jungles of Brazil at a cost of $300,000."

Lincoln carried off the role in grand style; the fact that he was far from a polished or accomplished actor only added to the realism in a film which badly needed it, as fans had little difficulty in distinguishing between the real animals and those impersonated by actors dressed in ingenious (for the time) ape suits devised by E. M. Jahraus of National's property department. To its credit, the original film was filled with well composed and thoughtfully photographed scenes (prints seen today have lost much of this quality by constant duping in which each new print looses some of the quality of its predecessor) and it proved to be a rousingly good adventure picture that made money by the carload in spite of the fact that its jungle setting (quite a novelty in 1918) was not authentic.

Elmo was convincing enough as the "Lord of the Jungle," but for those of you whose memory of Tarzan centers on a tree-swinging acrobat, it certainly wasn't Lincoln. His great bulk was a distinct liability in this respect and what swinging he did was kept to eight feet above the ground. But despite his size, Elmo proved to be sufficiently agile and his fight scenes were brutal and well done. For one-shot casting honors, whoever signed Lincoln for the role was certainly right on the mark. *The Romance of Tarzan* followed less than nine months later, with Elmo once again assuming the lead as Tarzan. Shot mainly in California, some of the footage taken in Louisiana during filming of the first feature was also incorporated, and while the critics were less than enthusiastic about stuffing the untamed hero into a dress suit, fans kept up a steady procession at the box-office.

On the strength of these two pictures, Elmo signed a contract with Universal for three serials and a feature, then reappeared once more as Tarzan in *The Adventures of Tarzan*, a 1921 serial. But Lincoln found his career had stopped in mid-stream. He was unable to find more leading roles, and after a small part in *The Hunchback of Notre Dame* (1923), he left the screen to prospect and speculate in Nevada's silver mines. He resumed his starring screen career in a 1927 Rayart serial, *King of the Jungle,* but it did not prove to be a comeback and he returned to Nevada until the early thirties, when he took another fling at acting.

Elmo's career was unfortunate in several aspects. His physique restricted the type and kind of roles he could handle successfully, his acting was awkward and selfconscious, but the largest factor was Elmo himself; and as much as any other reason, this kept him from the screen— he took his own publicity extremely seriously and proved far too temperamental for most directors to bother with. While filming *The Adventures of Tarzan,* director Robert F. Hill finally reached a point where he tried to avoid contact with Elmo because of their innumerable clashes. Recounting several of these episodes to me one evening some years ago, Bob Hill recalled that not until he hit upon the idea of threatening to kill off his main character at the 10th episode (it was a 15-chapter serial) was Elmo willing to cooperate—after Lincoln finally got the message, things went smoothly the rest of the way.

Much of his glory and all of the memories return to the years 1918–21, when Elmo reigned supreme as the "Lord of the Jungle"—his one and only great role. But to Lincoln, being the first of a long line of screen Tarzans had its own reward, and although fond of bitterly denouncing the shabby way Hollywood treated its own when they had passed their prime, Elmo was proud of his achievements, hanging on with occasional roles until his death while working as an extra in Charles Starrett's Columbia westerns in 1952.

Elmo Lincoln.

As Tarzan of the Apes, *his only important role in a brief starring career.*

TOMMY MEIGHAN

Dashing young heroes didn't fare too well on the silent screen until the latter twenties, when youngsters began to edge the adults out of the audience. Until that time, the mature leading man more than held his own. The neat and ever-dependable hero who could win with his head as well as his fists held the reins on the audiences' fancies and Tommy Meighan stood at the top of the class in this category. A native of Pittsburgh, Meighan had started in show business as an extra in *Mistress Nell,* spent three seasons working with David Warfield and reached Broadway on his 21st birthday in 1900.

Some sixteen years later, Paramount brought Tommy to the screen in *The Fighting Hope.* The advent of Triangle in the fall of 1915 had created a considerable market in filmdom for stage actors and Meighan willingly joined the exodus to the screen. His progress was slow at first but steady, and in 1919 he was cast as the racketeer hero of George Loane Tucker's production of *The Miracle Man.* A signal hit of the year, this film brought near-instant fame to both Meighan and another member of the cast, Lon Chaney.

Tommy's popularity increased considerably with his role in DeMille's *Male and Female,* an updated version of James Barrie's *The Admirable Crichton.* In this "daring" revelation of the intimate adventures of a lady of quality (Gloria Swanson) and her butler (Meighan) on a desert island, the emphasis was placed on sex and sin, and Tommy proved he was box-office material. Working for Paramount until 1929, he reached the height of his popularity in the mid-twenties without ever making a picture in Hollywood. Like a few other Paramount stars, Meighan refused to move West to the movie colony and did his work at the Astoria studio in the New York City borough of Queens.

By the early twenties, Meighan had married Frances Ring, a well-known stage actress, and was settled into the comfortable rut of one box-office success after another. His basic screen personality remained pretty much the same despite his variety of performances—as a romantic leading man, a melodramatic victim of the whimsey of life, a mobster redeemed by the innocence of a crippled girl, a no-account thrown out of town who returned years later to square matters. Tommy even did light comedy and this seeming versatility on his part kept his fans coming back for more even though he was well into his forties.

Historians and critics have paid little attention to Tommy Meighan over the years, and virtually every reference to him found in works dealing with the screen during the twenties merely mentions his name; a sad fate for one whose appeal lasted more than a decade. But then, Meighan's stardom isn't easy to explain. Many of his pictures were like *Manslaughter*—overwrought, overly melodramatic, and improbable slices of life which are no longer the impressive documents of the twenties that their box-office reception made them decades ago. Glossy and slick productions of their era, which are seldom revived today except by writers, many were pacesetters at the time, but have lost the glamor once associated with them.

In his history of the screen, *The Rise of the American Film,* Lewis Jacobs credited *The Miracle Man* as heralding the advent of an era in which materialism succeeded principles and *Male and Female* as symbolic of the new age in which sex, sin and sensationalism rose to supremacy on the screen. Tommy Meighan was right in the midst of this cinematic revolution, and while his reputation has long since diminished considerably in comparison to such contemporaries as John Gilbert, Lon Chaney and Valentino, he once stood high on the list of popular favorites. He led a quiet private life and needed no press agentry to help maintain his popularity with audiences his own age. The few of Meighan's films in existence today rest in the hands of private collectors or in archives and are rarely seen by the rank and file interested in the silent film, a neglect that has not helped his memory with newer generations.

Tommy worked into the sound era after leaving Paramount, but shortly after making *Peck's Bad Boy* for Sol Lesser in 1934, illness forced his retirement from the screen. Meighan entered the hospital and never recovered; it was a long road to travel that ended in a coma and death two years later in 1936 at the age of 57. His obituaries were brief and a public once fascinated with the exploits of this gruff-looking actor of Irish descent turned its attention elsewhere; Tommy Meighan was soon forgotten.

To those readers interested in the silent screen for its own worth, I highly recommend that should you ever have the opportunity to attend a revival of some of Tommy's work, don't miss it. Paradoxical though Meighan's career may have been, he was an important part of that era often referred to as the movies' golden age, and an interesting figure in his own right.

Thomas Meighan.

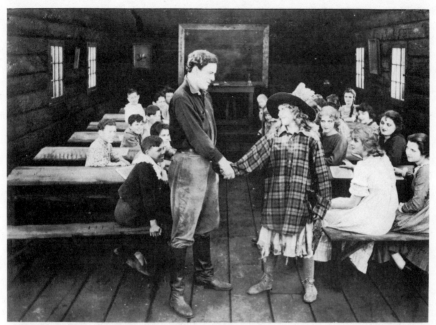

M'Liss *found Tommy supporting Paramount's top star, Mary Pickford,* in 1918.

Meighan and Leatrice Joy in Manhandled, 1922.

Tommy and Lila Lee in Male and Female, *1919.*

Guy Oliver, Tommy and Lois Wilson in Our Leading Citizen, 1922.

You can get a glimpse of Tommy's appeal in this publicity picture with Jack Dempsey and John McCormack.

Tommy on location for The Alaskan, *1924.*

With Lila Lee in The New Klondike, *1926.*

Meighan's pictures were well-staged and scenic but the ladies in the audience were mainly interested in Tommy.

With Renee Adoree in Tin Gods, *1926.*

Tommy and his wife, actress Frances Ring.

TONY MORENO

One of the great success stories of the motion picture came to a Spanish actor known as Tony Moreno. None would have ever guessed from watching this suave man of action who became a light-hearted lover in later screen adventures that Moreno's career was quite a quirk of fate, which had smiled kindly upon him in the person of two generous American tourists. Born in Madrid, Spain, in 1887, Antonio Garrido Montegudo was apprenticed to a baker when he was only nine years old. The garrulous young boy captivated the fancy of two wealthy Americans who had stopped by the baker's shop, and before they left Spain for the United States, he had been invited to join them in New York City. Arriving in this country, he was enrolled in school and given an education. While completing his schooling in Northampton, Massachusetts, young Moreno undertook a number of part time and odd jobs, one of which brought him into contact with a local theatre. Sent to repair a defect in the electrical wiring behind stage, Tony became enamored of the foot lights and decided to become an actor. And why not? Was anything impossible for a poor boy rescued from the clutches of a slave-driving baker?

Anthony Moreno's first screen appearance came in 1914 in a two-reeler for Rex, *The Voice of Millions,* and launched a career that was to make him well-known to every woman in America. Tony rose to fame at Vitagraph, where he eventually shared star status with Earle Williams and William Duncan for several years. His early roles in support of Van Dyke Brooks (bet you can't remember him!) were many and varied, but the dark-eyed, intense young man caught on quickly, and by World War I he was one of Vitagraph's two serial heroes. While William Duncan took care of the out-of-doors adventure fans, Tony complemented that casting by starring in *The Iron Test, The Perils of Thunder Mountain, The Invisible Hand* and *The Veiled Mystery*—all cliff-hanging chapter plays that mixed drawing room drama with adventure between 1918–20.

Moreno's career might well have moved considerably faster had he left Vitagraph at that time, but contented with working for Albert E. Smith and satisfied with his $3000 weekly salary, Tony's career as a leading man hung in suspended animation for some time. Of the pioneer production companies, Vitagraph alone had managed to survive the changing times and tastes, but despite its existence until 1925, major importance had bypassed the company and its productions long before. Tony came into his own at Paramount in mid-decade with choice roles in *The Trail of the Lonesome Pine, Midnight Taxi, Mare Nostrum* (for M-G-M), *Beverly of Graustark* and *It,* co-starring along the way with ladies like Marion Davies, Clara Bow, Alice Terry and even Garbo.

While others his age showed the advancing years and watched their careers gradually decline, Moreno was fortunate that he wore his years well, growing stronger in popularity and demand as the decade moved on. While not the dashing romantic hero cut from Valentino cloth, Moreno was nevertheless considered to be of the same general type and nearly found himself caught in the same mold. Only occasional appearances in adventurous roles like *The Border Legion* kept Tony from spending his entire starring career in the company of beautiful women.

Moreno made the transition to talkies with ease, but not as a leading man. Now it was character roles that came his way in abundance, for his slight accent ruined any hopes of his continuing as a star, and in a way this handicap worked to excellent advantage for the actor, who was well into his forties. At that age, he couldn't hope to conquer the sound screen as he had the silent, but once producers caught his accent, everyone seemed to remember at the same time that Tony Moreno spoke perfect Spanish. From roughly 1930 to 1935, Hollywood filmed its Spanish version at the same time the English version was made and during those five years, Moreno was in heavy demand as an actor (and sometime director), tearing from studio to studio and set to set to keep up with the filming schedules.

Having married wealth in the person of Daisy Canfield and having wisely invested his money, Moreno had amassed sufficient funds to easily carry him through 1936–41, when he totaled but 35 days before the camera in the five-year period. Once the simultaneous shooting schedules were abandoned, producers forgot that Tony could act as quickly as they had recalled that he could speak Spanish. Taking a high-flying fling at a real estate development named Moreno Highlands occupied part of his spare time and much of his fortune; it turned out to be a financial disaster that cost Tony several hundred thousand dollars.

The forties and fifties saw Moreno with few but choice roles in colorful epics like *Captain From Castile* and he worked until 1958, when retirement finally came after completion of a role in Gary Cooper's *Dallas*. Few moviegoers of that era recognized the one-time leading man as a former star in his own right, and fewer even recalled that Tony Moreno was still living. When he retired, Moreno granted interviews and jokingly referred to himself as a 59-year-old for whom there was no longer a place on the screen—looking all the while more like 59 than his real age of 72. When Tony passed away in 1967, the size of his million-dollar estate caused bitter disagreements among his heirs and brought the Cinderella story of a poor Spanish boy named Antonio Garrido Montegudo back into the limelight for one final brief moment.

Tony Moreno.

Tony and Colleen Moore in Look Your Best, *1923. Moreno had risen to fame at Vitagraph during the World War I years.*

Tony, Mary Miles Minter and Ernest Torrance in The Trail of the Lonesome Pine, *1923. This was Miss Minter's last film.*

Beverly of Graustark *paired Tony with Marion Davies in 1926.*

Tony accuses Alice Terry in Mare Nostrum, *1926.*

No drawing room idol, Tony took his share of punishment in many of his screen portrayals. This is from The Temptress *in 1926, Garbo's second American picture.*

Fantasy with Hedda Hopper and Julanne Johnston in Venus of Venice, 1927.

Tony had the best of two worlds in Adoration, 1929. *Serious acting . . .*

. . . as well as moment of dalliance with Billie Dove.

He-man roles such as Romance of the Rio Grande *in 1929 had kept Tony from being typecast as a romantic idol. Here he's about to settle a grudge with Warner Baxter.*

Tony's age was still well hidden in 1929, when he made Careers *with Billie Dove. This was her first talkie.*

RAMON NOVARRO

The director of Metro's *The Four Horsemen of the Apocalypse,* in which Rudolph Valentino came to public attention, Rex Ingram was also responsible for the stardom of one Jose Ramon Gil Samaniegos, who made female hearts beat quite a bit faster in the twenties as Ramon Novarro. Ingram, who held little fondness for the Latin lover he had created, maintained that Valentino's talent was only incidental in his sudden rise to fame. Claiming that the story and director were more responsible, he ventured the opinion that he could make a star of any clean-cut, good-looking youngster. To prove it, he selected a virtually unknown Mexican-born actor to play the roguish Rupert of Hentzau in *The Prisoner of Zenda* (1923) and indeed made him a star. But this effort solved nothing for Ingram, who then found himself involved in disagreements about the likelihood of Novarro's stardom with and without the director's help.

But to Ramon Novarro, the role and his subsequent fame meant a great deal. Ramon had been born into a large family whose middle class life was disrupted in 1913 by revolution. His father left the turbulence of life in Mexico for a new start in the United States, but America was not kind to him and he never regained the lifestyle that he had enjoyed in Mexico. Ramon himself was unable to find little more than odd jobs —grocery clerk, theatre usher, piano teacher, cafe singer—until a dance director, Marion Morgan, arranged to have him included in her vaudeville act. This eventually paved the way to movies, where Ramon found mostly obscure bits like the gladiator in *A Small Town Idol,* a 1921 Ben Turpin comedy, but with his appearance in *The Rubaiyat of Omar Khayyam,* Novarro caught Rex Ingram's eye, and when the director cast him as the lead in *The Prisoner of Zenda,* Ingram was actually hedging his bet. He had recognized talent in young Novarro and planned to develop it. Following this role with *Scaramouche,* Ramon's success was secure; this second performance under Ingram proved that his acclaim was no accident.

Valentino had left M-G-M for Paramount after a salary dispute, but the studio still had two extremely popular leading men in Ramon and Jack Gilbert. Competing on the screen with Jack and Rudy was a pretty heady challenge and one that Novarro never entirely conquered, but for once the studio had made the correct decision—to pit Ramon against Valentino as another smoldering Latin would be a foolish move and so Ramon was gradually moved to modern adventure stories. But his greatest hit rested in a period picture that nearly broke M-G-M's financial back.

George Walsh had been sent to Italy to play the lead in *Ben Hur,* but a series of drawn-out, expensive errors and misjudgments (both on location and in the home office) dictated a change in directors and this cost Walsh his role; Novarro was sent to Italy to replace him. Few roles stand out in the minds of moviegoers old enough to remember with the vividness of Novarro's on-screen duel with the wicked Messala, played by veteran Francis X. Bushman, who was having a field day acting rings around the newcomer when Louis B. Mayer stepped in and restored a balance. *Ben Hur* benefited from the reams of publicity during its long filming, and like so many other silent films has been imitated but never since equalled. A good portion of the film's intensity and depth came from the performances of Novarro and Bushman. While Ramon made several other interesting pictures—*Trifling Woman, Where the Pavement Ends, The Arab, Mata Hari*—during his career, one seems to remember only *Ben Hur.*

Years later, Ramon was prone to contradicting himself in scores of interviews as to what had made him a great star; on one hand, he credited the deliberate, intense and quiet manner of romantic lovemaking that had endeared him to his loyal fans (Novarro's fan club operated for years after he left the screen, publishing a regular bulletin of the star's activities and philosophies) but at the same time, he was just as apt to credit his success to a careful choice of camera angles, calculated movements and the repeated use of one basic story, pointing out that this would work for anyone during the silent era.

More fortunate than Jack Gilbert, who found the transition to talkies impossible, Ramon was cast in *The Pagan,* and singing "The Pagan Love Song," he successfully launched himself into sound. But as the romantic epic with which he was best identified quickly passed from public favor in the early thirties, Novarro turned to other roles and despite the criticism of some earlier in his career, Ramon proved he could act. But by 1938, Novarro concluded that he and the screen had seen their best days together and he retired to a quiet life of leisure. He traveled, lectured, dabbled in real estate and lived the unassuming life of a retired bachelor until the late fifties, when he began playing character roles on television shows like *Combat*.

Suddenly Novarro found himself in demand once again. It wasn't star billing, but the parts were juicy and he began with a caution he soon discarded, undertaking a full schedule of such roles and turning in performances that kept producers coming back again and again. Years had passed, and although the fan clubs had long disbanded, a sufficient number of his faithful remained. Letters began arriving again and gradually the name Ramon Novarro took on a new complexion—here was one of the romantic idols of the twenties who was more than just a memory, he was really an actor.

Ramon's new career came to a tragic close in 1969 when he was found murdered in his modest home, the victim of a senseless slaying. Unlike many of the other silent screen heroes, Ramon can still be seen at his best in a number of television shows occasionally rerun in recent years, even though his big hits of the past are still locked in M-G-M's vault (those that haven't deteriorated beyond rescue). It's likely that the unassuming Novarro would rather be remembered for the choice bits and pieces than the glossy whole, but then it would be fun to watch him romp through *Scaramouche* once more.

Ramon Novarro.

Director Rex Ingram was convinced that he could take a virtual unknown and make him a star, as he had done with Valentino. He selected Ramon, shown here in Trifling Women *with Barbara La Marr in 1922.*

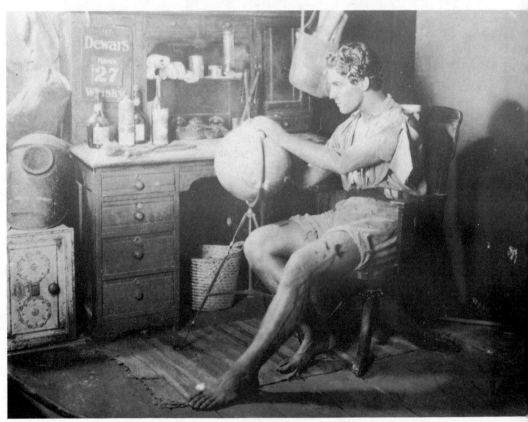

Where the Pavement Ends, *1923.*

Rex Ingram, Ramon and Curt Rikfeld (assistant director and production manager) during the filming of Scaramouche *at the Metro studio on Cahuenga and Romaine in 1923.*

Ramon, Wallace Beery and Enid Bennett in The Red Lily, 1924.

Ramon replaced George Walsh in the role of Ben Hur, 1927. This was his most famous performance.

With Norma Talmadge in The Student Prince, *1927.*

Ramon made the transition to talkies with The Pagan, *1930.*

Call of the Flesh, *a 1930 talkie with Dorothy Jordan.*

HERBERT RAWLINSON

Several silent screen actors became very well known, acquired a large following of fans and played leading roles for many years without ever really achieving stardom or significant recognition in the ranks of their profession. They were steady, dependable box-office draws around whom low-budget pictures could be constructed, and because of this wide attraction they really formed the backbone of the industry's growth. One such was an Englishman who arrived in the United States around 1910 to assume the management of the Belasco Stock Company, Herb Rawlinson.

He soon discovered that the rapidly growing cinema offered more financial rewards than the operation of the stock company and went to work at Selig in 1911, appearing first in *The Novice.* Herb was successful enough at Selig, but a chance to join Universal meant more money and so he became one of the growing list of converts to Carl Laemmle's employ. In 1915, Rawlinson made his first big splash as the hero of a 15-episode chapter play, *The Black Box,* in which he played a variation on the scientific detective theme made popular by Arthur B. Reeve's fictional character, Craig Kennedy. *The Black Box* was popular enough with cliffhanger fans but Herb returned to short dramas and occasional features until he made *The Carter Case* with Marguerite Marsh in 1919, this time playing Craig Kennedy.

Herb's screen character as it evolved in the early twenties was skillfully concocted to take advantage of the best of two worlds; he was usually seen as the gay young blade with slightly foppish manners whose top hat and tails concealed the fact that he was only too willing to take them off, roll up his sleeves and defend his honor, or that of any lady in the vicinity. With his wavy brown hair and soft blue eyes, Herb made an ideal gentleman of quality; tall, slender and attractively handsome, his broad grin was a comforting sight to any helpless heroine.

The Rawlinson image, with its half-frozen smile (or scowl, as the occasion warranted), was a familiar sight on the screen almost to the

end of the twenties. When Herb wasn't working in Universal programmers, he was starring in independent pictures or serials. Fans could
predict the plots of Herb's films with ease: boy meets girl, falls in love,
girl is in trouble, boy solves problem, and both live happily ever after.
Pure corn by today's standards, but it was a staple diet demanded by
audiences of a half-century or so ago, and with dependable leading men
like Herb around, producers were glad to oblige.

Herb never made any big pictures in his career, but he always seemed
to be in demand and worked steadily in the formula pictures. About the
only real variation came in the guise of his portrayals; while often
seen as a society dandy in romantic melodrama, he also played police
officers out to redeem the tough neighborhood, firemen battling to save
the department's reputation, or undercover agents masquerading as play-
boys. Regardless, there was more than a healthy amount of romantic
interest included and while Herb seldom swept the leading lady off her
feet in Valentino fashion, he did manage to spend a great deal of time
smiling at her with adoring eyes and flashing teeth; Rawlinson had one
of the most delightful stock grins in the business.

While many of Herb's pictures called for manly action in the face
of danger, his fight scenes were usually staged rather poorly, involving
a good deal of pushing and shoving, although the accompanying still
pictures give the impression that he was quite adept at self-defense.
Several of Herb's pictures of the twenties are still in circulation today
and prove quite disappointing when screened some four or five decades
after they were made. In his long career before the camera, Rawlinson
worked for just about everyone, from First National, Goldwyn, Paramount and M-G-M to Universal and the independents; for actors like
Herb there always seemed to be a role waiting in the wings and he kept
as busy as anyone could want to, well into his forties.

Sound took the edge from Herb's career and the hero of countless
screen adventures quit the screen without fanfare in 1929 to return to
the stage, where he stayed for a decade, with only occasional character
roles in talkies during the thirties. A scattering of screen jobs came his
way after that, but Herb spent the war years and after mainly in radio.
His delightful English voice found a ready market in the golden years
of broadcasting and he was in near-constant demand for top radio shows
like the Lux Theatre.

Herb Rawlinson passed away from lung cancer in 1953, just as the
type of hero he had so often portrayed was passing from the screen.
The program pictures were fighting a losing battle with increasing costs
and declining receipts and their golden years were far behind. But Herb

had been there at their beginning and as the B picture came into its own in the twenties, so had he. His was a style of entertainment that never varied, yet audiences enjoyed the programmers for over thirty years and with their popularity rested the screen career of a gentlemanly actor who was always ready to fill in those unbooked play dates between Ramon Novarro and Milton Sills. Although he was never a major screen star, Herb's fans kept him at work for years. No actor can exist for very long without an audience but Herbert Rawlinson had little to worry about—he just went from picture to picture and many of us went along with him at the time.

Herbert Rawlinson.

Herb and Elaine Davis in an early Selig, The Liar, *circa 1912.*

Herb throws a beautiful punch for the still photographer's benefit in High Speed, *1920.*

Rawlinson's heroics occasionally took him out of evening clothes.

Herb just couldn't seem to stay out of trouble. Here's a fight scene from
The Prisoner, *1923.*

Rawlinson spent more time trading punches than embracing the girls—that's why the kids loved him.

Herb's talkie roles were small and far apart, and he left movies for radio and the Lux Theatre. This is from Fred MacMurray's Men Without Names, 1935.

CHARLES RAY

In this day and age of the anti-hero as screen star, it's a bit difficult to look back and imagine the rustic small town boy as a popular leading character, yet a rural America that has since all but disappeared once held a fascination for screen audiences and no one profited more from this than a moonfaced juvenile named Charles Ray. Ray had joined Thomas H. Ince around 1912, after playing scores of juvenile roles with countless traveling stock companies and soon carved out a place on the screen as Ince's foremost exponent of youthful vigor. His early roles like that of the mountain boy *In the Tennessee Hills* demanded an outward strength of character that became submerged once he reached stardom in *The Coward;* from that point on, Ray projected more like the apologetic youngster who tried his best to overcome adversity and fate with nothing more than good deeds and intentions.

People pushed him around without much effort until grit and determination finally rose up to strike down his detractors like vengeful lightning in the final reel. In a sense, he reflected a personality type greatly admired during the World War I years (old timers called it character) and somewhat of a variation on the Horatio Alger theme. Charlie was kind, polite and generous to a fault, traits easily taken advantage of, but whereas Alger's heroes immediately dealt with double-dealing as such situations arose, Charlie always put off the reckoning as long as possible. But when he did settle the score, it was always in his favor regardless of the degree of previous torments.

Charlie came roaring to attention for his sensitive portrayal in *The Coward,* a 1915 Ince drama that featured ambivalent attitudes toward the Civil War. As a Southern lad who did not wish to participate in the grand slaughter, he was forced into military service by a dour father, one whose fondest recollections were those of his soldiering days, and until the middle of the film when Charlie deserted to return home, the emphasis was decidedly anti-war. But once Ray had obtained the Northern battle plan and learned that his father had joined the regiment to serve in his place, the emphasis turned to patriotism, and in a moving finale that saw father unwittingly shoot son (not fatally), the picture seemed to preach understanding and tolerance. While Frank Keenan (as the father) had been billed as the lead, *The Coward* was definitely young Ray's picture, and brought in by director Reginald Barker at a negative cost of only $17,922.87, it proved to be a huge money-maker.

From this point on, Charlie's screen image never seemed to vary a great deal from that of *The Coward;* his best pictures were pastoral symphonies in which he projected as a sensitive lad whose self-doubt and easy-going manner made an ideal target for every bully in the neighborhood. Yet thanks to his scriptwriters, courage eventually surged into his veins and right triumphed over its natural enemy. Don't knock it—it was good for $11,000 weekly at a time when income taxes were a joke.

Some have suggested that Charlie might have retained his popularity a good deal longer had he attempted to add more dimension to his screen character, but looking at Ray's career in the twenties, we see each such attempt meet with failure. Charlie's own personality abounded with the same quality of naïveté that he portrayed so well on-screen One of the first of the movie millionaires to move into Beverly Hills, Charlie just assumed that solid gold door knobs were in good taste and never seemed able to understand why people with whom he associated thought him just a bit peculiar for dressing formally with his wife before sitting down to partake of the evening meal (every evening of the year in formal dress?).

Ray left Tom Ince in 1921, ostensibly because he was tired of playing one character, and opened his own studio. Hit after hit continued to flash on the screen until he had resisted change to a point where he could no longer afford to look the other way. Public tastes were moving away from the image he played so well and Charlie decided to sink everything into his own production of colonial America, *The Courtship of Miles Standish*. Investing all of his own funds and everything he could possibly borrow, Ray translated the famed poem to the screen. It took two hours to view the finished product, and in that 120 minutes, Charles Ray became a pauper.

A total failure, *The Courtship of Miles Standish* cost Ray his fortune and his credit, practically wiping out his stardom at the same time. Moving to the other extreme with city slicker and society playboy roles (like that of Corinne Griffith's *The Garden of Eden* in 1928), proved an equally bad move, for even though he was garbed in sophisticated adult clothes, Charlie still came across as the small town boy of *The*

Busher and *Hay Foot, Straw Foot* in appearance and mannerisms, only further removed from his own environment.

Ray's problem was partially one of personality and partially one of ability. He didn't like to be told what others thought had made him a star, but try as he might, Charlie simply seemed unable to shake the mold in which he had been cast. By the latter twenties, he was no longer an important star, but rather one of those unfortunate souls who had tasted the heady wine of stardom only to watch the golden goblet leak at an increasingly frenzied and unrepairable pace until the wine was gone forever.

Unfortunately, Charlie never really discovered what had collapsed his career, and he greeted the declining years with an amazement that was difficult to disguise. In between picture assignments, he tried his hand at running a flower shop, a book shop, tried to start a magazine and even wrote and published a couple of books, but to no avail. He found work in 1936 as a non-speaking extra in *Hollywood Boulevard* at $7.50 and shortly after fell victim to a nervous condition. Charlie entered a hospital and was not seen on the screen until 1941, but a comeback at that time was quite out of the question. In 1943, he developed an infection from an impacted tooth and died five weeks after entering Cedars of Lebanon in Hollywood, a lonely and destitute man.

But for a few years and under the guiding hand of Tom Ince, Charles Ray had hit it big and to almost all devotees of the silent screen today, his name conjures up visions of a less complicated and far happier time, when a country boy with a straw hat and fish pole could be a hero to millions of screen fans and an idol to a generation who sincerely believed in the ideals that Charlie had brought to life before their very eyes.

Charles Ray.

Ray and W. H. Thompson in a 1916 Triangle, The Dividend.

Ray's country boy portrayals began at Triangle under Thomas H. Ince.

As the small town lad who eventually made good, Charles Ray amassed a fortune. When the characterization began to fail him, Charlie turned to history and a poem for subject matter—both virtually ruined him. But in 1919, he was riding high in The Egg Crate Wallop.

Tender scenes like this from Paris Green captivated rural America of 1920, which still placed great stock in the old-fashioned virtues, and Ray represented them all.

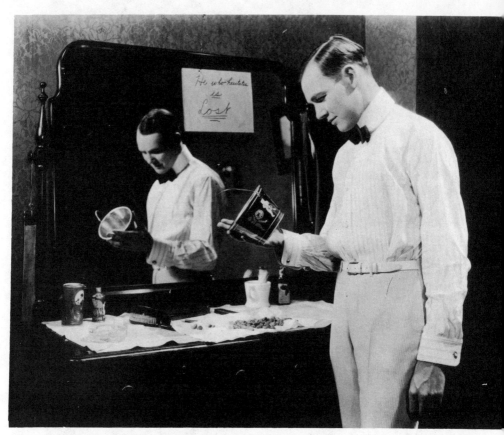

Alarm Clock Andy *and Charles Ray were synonymous in 1920; both were of an era fast disappearing.*

One of Ray's final rural heroes from The Girl I Loved, 1923. *This adaptation from the poem by James Whitcomb Riley may have given the star the idea that he could successfully translate* The Courtship of Miles Standish *to the screen.*

This publicity pose was taken after the release of The Courtship of
Miles Standish *in 1924 and while there's probably no connection, it did
represent Ray's financial state of affairs.*

Charlie tried his luck in man-of-the-world parts like this scene with Leatrice Joy from Vanity *in 1927, but less than successful, Ray went into the thirties bewildered at his failure to regain the immense popularity he had known a decade before.*

WALLACE REID

The extreme popularity of Wallace Reid was one of the genuine phenomena of the silent screen, and looking back from the vantage point of a half-century, it's sometimes difficult to believe that he made such a lasting impression in such a short time without any pictures to his credit that could be considered as classics of the screen. When Wally Reid died of narcotics addiction January 18, 1923, a shocked nation slipped into national mourning for the young idol and the Hays office gained a great deal of strength in its attempt to regulate the screen. The scandal surrounding his death followed closely upon the unsolved murder of director William Desmond Taylor and the Roscoe Arbuckle case.

The son of stage actor Hal Reid, Wally was born in St. Louis and educated in New York City. He worked in vaudeville with his father in *The Girl and the Ranger,* and when Hal Reid transferred his attention to the movies in 1911, Wally went along with him. Until 1915, young Reid worked as an actor, writer and sometime assistant director—a sort of general utility man who could fill in wherever necessary. Wally had little desire to become an actor; he much preferred to be behind the camera, but an interview with D. W. Griffith changed the course of his career in 1915.

Griffith had summoned Wally with the avowed intention of casting him in the role later played by Henry B. Walthall in *The Birth of a Nation;* and after the interview, Reid knew that he had secured a role and assumed that it was to be that of the lead, but when filming began, he discovered he was to play the blacksmith in a single sequence. Griffith put down all protests by telling Wally that his particular role would do more for his career, and as usual D. W. proved to be correct, an attribute that made many feel that the director was an insufferable snob. When *The Birth* was released, Griffith began to receive fan mail asking about the young man who portrayed the fighting blacksmith and Wally Reid was on his way; he worked in several of Griffith's Fine

Arts productions at Triangle and then left to join Famous Players.

Wally was youthful, athletic and rather handsome with a whimsical, winning personality that contained the intrinsic qualities that made stars of unknowns in those days; and his strong personal magnetism extended to a screen image that captivated everyone in the audience, men and women alike. For the most part, he played the virtuous young American male on-screen—the soda clerk who made good, a daredevil auto racer, an ambitious salesman—all with an affable air of optimism. These qualities were but an extension of his off-screen personality, for Wally Reid was as popular with his co-workers and acquaintances as he was with audiences. During the time he was afflicted with the narcotics problem, everyone who worked around Wally realized that he was not well, but very few learned the reason why until the very end; even with all of his own troubles, Wally was solicitous of his fellow man and never exercised his temperament as a star.

With all this working in his favor, one would have thought that Paramount would have capitalized on it by starring Wally in pictures worthy of his considerable appeal and talent, but instead he was worked very hard in a large number of films that are best described as pleasant little programmers, few of them really worthy of his presence. Wally had the good fortune (in a sense of the word) of being at home in costume dramas, outdoor roles, comedy and outright farce; he played all these roles with a believable vigor that caught the fancy of moviegoers. As a result, none of his starring work was really worthy of his presence yet all were box-office attractions. Hollywood would earn a well-deserved notoriety for its exploitation of talent like Wally's with little regard for the human consequences.

His initial exposure to drugs has been the topic of a large variety of differing stories over the years. Some say his addiction stemmed from the result of an accident, while others claim it was the consequence of his association with certain directors and actors, but the most likely version is also the least dramatic. Wally was rushing from picture to picture, working long hard hours to keep up the pace when an accident on the set resulted in a back injury. Morphine was administered to keep him going and by the time he was able to seek medical attention, it was too late. Wally had been on drugs for over a year when he collapsed mid-way through the production of *Mr. Billings Spends His Dime* in 1922. Quitting work, he went for a brief rest in the mountains before committing himself to a sanitarium where he hoped to effect a cure; Walter Hiers replaced him in the picture and nothing was said about the incident.

The public was unaware of Reid's unfortunate affliction until just before Christmas 1922, when his family announced that Wally was a victim of drugs. The outpouring of national sympathy was unbelievable, and to an adoring public Wally announced that he would win the fight; but less than a month later the end came from lung and kidney congestion. In a large sense, the studio shared responsibility for what had happened to Wally Reid, but as it did in Roscoe Arbuckle's case, Paramount tried to turn its eyes away. To mollify Reid's large following of devout fans, the studio announced that it would erect a memorial in his memory. Three years later nothing had been done, and so the Wallace Reid Memorial Club was organized to help remind Paramount of its promise; but the furor had dissipated by then and no memorial ever came into being.

Wally's pictures were reportedly destroyed by studio executives who no longer wished to be involved, although prints of a few did survive in his wife's care. As Reid made so many in such a short time, their quality varied greatly but all seemed to share one thing in common— a lack of real substance. That Wally Reid was able to carry the heavy burden placed upon him by a superhuman schedule of inexpensive pictures virtually on the strength of his personality (few had any real plots, just situations) is a tribute to what this fine young actor might have done had he been given worthwhile stories with which to work. That he acquired a large and fanatically loyal following in spite of his pictures is an even greater tribute to Wallace Reid.

As those who recall his starring years pass on, the memory of Wally lingers mainly because of the tragic circumstances of his death at 30; but the real tragedy of Wallace Reid came with his exploitation by a major studio as a vein of gold to be mined for profit, depriving his fans and the entertainment medium in which he worked of the real and considerable talents this versatile young actor could have brought to bear on roles worthy of him. For this neglect Paramount stands indicted.

Wallace Reid at home with his wife, actress Dorothy Davenport.

Wally and Mae Murray in To Have and to Hold, *1916.*

Under arrest in Joan the Woman, *1916.*

Wally and Ann Little in The Firefly of France, *1918.*

Wally in another costume drama, The Woman God Forgot, 1917. *These roles with Geraldine Farrar in DeMille's pictures were among his best dramas, but the camera spent most of its time focused on the Diva.*

Reid was also adept at light comedy, as in Sick Abed, 1920.

Raymond Hatton, Elliott Dexter, DeMille, Wally, Theodore Roberts and Monte Blue in a casual moment on the set of The Affairs of Anatol, 1921.

Reid's adventurous roles like Across the Continent, 1922, *made him popular with all audiences. Here he's in a Ford Special racer.*

WILL ROGERS

Destined to become the comic conscience of a nation desperately working to enjoy itself in the twenties, a rope-spinning Oklahoma cowboy named Will Rogers had conquered show business long before he arrived on the Goldwyn lot in 1918 to make his motion picture debut in *Laughing Bill Hyde.* Will appeared ill at ease and even awkward in his movies, but the down-home sincerity of his many Goldwyn pictures made him "one of the folks" and audiences warmed to him almost at once. While he often played the lead in these feature comic-dramas, Rogers was seen as often as a kindly advisor to Cullen Landis or other Goldwyn juveniles. Whatever the story line started out as, there was always a bend in the road that allowed Will his moments of pathos—an orphan boy, a homeless waif, a hungry destitute.

Will never really considered himself just a "movie actor" and between pictures, he performed on stage or on the road. A couple of years after shaking Sam Goldwyn's hand goodbye, Will turned up in Culver City with a contract bearing Hal Roach's signature and good for a series of short comedies. In between, he had stopped at Hodkinson to make a delightful screen version of Washington Irving's "The Legend of Sleepy Hollow" entitled *The Headless Horseman.*

The homespun philosopher had free creative rein during the production of the Roach short subjects, and it's for these comedies that he's best remembered on the silent screen. Satire and parody were Will's stock-in-trade, and he brought them to bear heavily in the Roach comedies, which seemed to break down into four areas of interest. A few were nonsensical monuments to whimsy (*Just Passing Through, Hustlin' Hank*). In comedies like *The Cake Eater,* which found Will as the shiftless ranch foreman whose masculinity overwhelmed the two spinster sisters visiting their property for the first time, and *Hustlin' Hank,* the rustic story of a ranch hand pressed into service as a photographer of nature studies, Rogers was out of his element and appeared to be going through the slapstick motions because he had to. One can almost imagine

Will in the screening room watching such comedies and inquiring of the director, "That's funny?"

Several ribbed the movies themselves (*Uncensored Movies, Big Moments From Little Pictures, Two Wagons—Both Covered*), with Will doing passable imitations of Doug Fairbanks imitating Robin Hood, William S. Hart imitating a cowboy, and the Keystone Kops imitating themselves. *Two Wagons—Both Covered* retold the epic western story of *The Covered Wagon* as Will felt it should have been made in the first place. Such lighthearted joshing at the movies as an institution came at a time when the entire industry was still rocking from the series of scandals which had befallen it in 1921–22. While the nation's press was doing its best to convince the American public that Hollywood was really Sodom in disguise, Will satirized it in the same way that he did Congress and Washington.

Many of his comedies dealt with his favorite topic—politics. These followed the adventures of his own political creation, Alfalfa Doolittle, through the inner workings of government, beginning with his election in *Alfalfa Doolittle,* his move to Washington and learning to play the pastime of all successful politicians, golf, in *Our Congressman.* Will was very much at home in subjects like *A Truthful Liar,* which gave him the opportunity to portray a rural politician returning home to his constituents to impress them with how hard he had worked in their behalf. As the story unfolded visually for the audience, the humorist was able to convey his impression of stock political phrases as used by the subtitles to describe the events being recounted and audiences were treated to the many subtle connotations such phrases carried.

Alfalfa Doolittle was Will's combination of two political creatures, the rural hayseed whose slow deliberation and lack of genuine ability seemed quite suitable for the ponderous workings of Washington, and the self-made folk hero whose "I was born in a log cabin" background had proven itself a formidable vote-getter dating from Civil War days. While Abner reflected no particular individual, he aptly summed up Will's oft-voiced impression of politicians in general, appearing more as a genuine incompetent than as a malicious conniver out to fleece his fellow man. Doolittle was the sum total of human frailty as Will saw it, one of a collection kept on periodic public display in the nation's capital to provide the newspapers with something to print, and changed every two years as the result of a marathon nationwide popularity contest.

Viewing these political satires today, one does not have to be very conversant with the politics of the twenties to recognize that Will managed to endow Abner Doolittle with a healthy amount of eternal truth.

The manner of speech and modes of dress may have changed in the intervening half-century, but Abner and his adventures in government continue to echo through the country today with as much validity as in the twenties.

Extracting material from the times in which he lived, material that seems even more pertinent now, Will concentrated heavily on social and environmental problems in his comedies. One genuine classic from this group remains—*Don't Park There*. Satirizing what Henry's Ford had done to the United States, and the developing traffic problem in the twenties, this comedy followed the headaches of a not-too-bright farmer who headed into town with his horse in search of medicine. On the way, he swapped the horse for a Tin Lizzy, spending the rest of the comedy driving around the country looking for a parking place. For those who enjoy picking such films apart completely for this hidden social significance (if any), the collapse of our hero's car at the close can be interpreted not only as a well-worn comic gag, but as Will's personal commentary on the increasing shoddiness of mass-produced goods.

But Will's forte during those years was really stand-up comedy and as the silent screen substituted pantomime for speech, much of the real humor in his Roach comedies came from the outrageous parody contained in the extremely clever subtitles which conveyed the effect Rogers desired. In some cases, the actual screen image was incidental to the titles, which made the necessary points all by themselves. As a screen comic, Will was often amusing, even interesting, but his work had little effect upon the screen and hardly ranked him among the comedy greats of the twenties. He was more of a recognized personality than a comedy star.

Will left the screen in 1924 when his Roach series ended and did not return until 1929, when he signed with Fox to become one of the best-loved comedians of the early talkie era. Playing such lovable characters as a pig farmer, country doctor, tramp and horse dealer, Will's personality projected with the same simplicity that characterized him in real life. With sound, Will Rogers became a star of the first magnitude and when he died in that 1935 airplane crash, he was earning $200,000 a picture. Unlike other screen actors who could be interchanged one among the other without notice, Will Rogers was one of a kind—there was no one to take his place and no one did.

Will Rogers.

Will came to the screen in 1918 with Laughing Bill Hyde *for Goldwyn.*

Will, Cullen Landis and Peggy Wood in Almost a Husband, *1919.*

Cupid, the Cowpuncher, *1920.*

The Cake Eater, *with Patsy O'Byrne.*

Will parodied Doug Fairbanks as Robin Hood in Big Moments from
Little Pictures, *one of his Roach comedies.*

MILTON SILLS

Some sixty years after it first began, the American public's love affair
with its movie stars has virtually ended. Few screen performers of today
enjoy the same intense idol worship that had characterized motion picture
stardom just a few decades ago and of the new breed of stars (if they
can even be called that), one wonders if their reputations will survive
beyond their mortality. It appears as if the seventies will be the age of
the anti-star, as the sixties were preoccupied by the anti-hero; and while
the present group of male performers are pleasant enough (and even
talented in a few cases), the public no longer holds a strong or even loyal
attachment to the majority. But it wasn't always that way.

Take a quick look at a husky fellow named Milton Sills to see what
I mean. Born in 1882 in Chicago and educated at the University of
Chicago, he was both a fellow and instructor in philosophy for a time.
Sills came to the screen in 1915 after a lengthy stage career as a leading
man for Belasco, Shubert, Frohman and William A. Brady—all among
the outstanding stage producers of their day. It was Brady who brought
Milton to his World Pictures after watching the actor perform for a week
on-stage, but Sills really established his screen career at Fox the following
year with a dramatic plea for prison reform in *The Honor System,* a role
that ignited a bright halo of stardom lasting right up to his death in 1930.

His extensive stage background gave the actor a firm grasp on audiences (mainly women, who were prone to carrying a crush for a lengthy
time after watching Milton in action) and he played every imaginable
role, from swashbucklers to westerns, melodrama to comedy, with equal
success and conviction. The ladies carried postcard portraits of his profile
in their purses and even the men had to agree that Sills was their kind
of screen hero, although they weren't too happy about his magical hold
on their wives. While Sills has often been characterized as a popular
version of the dignified and cultured John Barrymore, and one whose
films stood the test of audiences that frowned on Barrymore, this evalua-
tion isn't quite fair to him. Milton was a star in his own right whose

pictures often exceeded those of Barrymore in action and adventure while giving his whimsical wit and grace full range of expression; I'll concede the point that Barrymore was a finer actor. Although their idol has been gone for four decades now, Sills's fans still abound in large numbers, and while their ranks are thinning more each year, there's still an intense loyalty attached to the gentlemanly actor in the memories of the "Geritol Set" that has kept him high in their estimation for these many years.

Unfortunately, the films of Milton Sills are rare in number these days, and those that do exist are closely guarded in private collections, either for copyright or personal reasons. The much-heralded search of the American Film Institute for its "lost" films may well turn up some of Sills's pictures, a tantalizing thought for those who do remember him, and a potential educational experience for those who would like to learn what screen acting was all about. Milton's adventure pictures ranged from well-mounted minor epics like *The Sea Hawk,* a rollicking costume drama that allowed him to play a dual role, to *The Hawk's Nest,* a melodramatic story of Chinatown in which our hero surgically changed his identity to secure a confession that proved him innocent of murder—hardly significant pictures from a social standpoint, but darn good entertainment and well worth seeing again today.

Sills was off to a promising start in talkies with *The Sea Wolf* when he collapsed and died while playing tennis in 1930. It was typical of Sills that when he suffered the first pains in his chest, he knew what they were; but the actor insisted on finishing the game and he did. Doctors had warned him that his heart was not strong enough to continue the strenuous pace of living in which he engaged but Milton wasn't the type to settle back in an easy chair and retire at the peak of his career.

Occasional mention of his name today brings forth a small but vehement outpouring of affection from those old enough to remember; just the other night, I mentioned his name to a lady whose quick response was a heartfelt, "he was my first screen love affair." What better memory could any actor ask?

Milton Sills as The Sea Hawk, *1924.*

The Stronger Vow, *with Geraldine Farrar in 1919.*

Was there ever a more masculine hero than Milton in Burning Sands, *1922?*

Sills with Lois Wilson in Miss Lulu Bett, *1921.*

With Anna Q. Nilsson and Pauline Garon in Adam's Rib, *1923.*

Check that look of determination in Sills's eyes; Betty Bronson can only see Paradise, *1926.*

Milton upset the social event in Burning Daylight, 1928, *by using Guinn Williams and Arthur Stone to demonstrate how dogsleds work.*

The Hawk's Nest, *with his wife Doris Kenyon in 1928.*

RUDOLPH VALENTINO

Although it's dimmed somewhat in recent years, the legend of
Rudolph Valentino lives on as symbolic both of the silent screen and
a golden age of the motion picture. Reams of copy have been written
about the itinerant Italian gardener-dancer who rose from obscurity to
overnight stardom in 1921, reigning supreme as *the* male star for a brief
five years, only to pass away unexpectedly at the apex of an amazing
career. His death plunged a shocked nation into momentary mourning
for an idol whom detractors (and there were many) believed to possess
feet of clay.

Upon reexamination today, his films fail to really convey what all the
commotion was really about during 1921–26 and leave those whose
memories cannot reach back that far wondering just how unsophisticated
mother and grandmother must have been. Certainly Rudy sold sex on
the screen, but it was an aura of sex compounded with mystery and concocted to a great extent within the audiences' own imaginations; not the
flagrant and open sexual activity flaunted on today's screen by less-
talented personalities.

One must admit that for his time, Valentino was a super salesman;
with little more than a bare chest and a pair of smouldering eyes peering
out from under neatly slicked-back hair, he managed to instill the promise of passion in his most famous starring role, *The Sheik,* and pass the
title into the vernacular of the day. The power of the screen to impress,
mold and fashion both attitudes and opinions has escaped many otherwise
observant citizens, yet it does exist and when one considers the mentality
at which most successful screenplays (both past and present) have been
addressed, it becomes a frightening thought that such power could rest
in the hands or eyes of a nonentity like Rudy.

Eighteen-year old Rodolfo Alfonzo Raffaelo Pierre Filibert Guglielmi
de Valentino d'Antonguolla had arrived from Italy in 1913 with very
little money, few skills and no idea of any particular career in mind.
It was enough just to be in America and one odd job after another

appeared to be sufficient to keep body and soul together, although Rudy seemed to have more of a flair for gardening than anything else. Except for dancing. Dancing was not only a love but a passion with the young man, and in the days of vaudeville it was easy enough for a good hoofer to find work.

Dancing eventually brought Valentino to Hollywood, where friends like Mae Murray urged him to try motion pictures. He did, but little resulted in an era that saw rural homespun America predominant on the screen in the persons of Charles Ray and Richard Barthelmess. Rudy's appearance was a lightyear's distance from that type, and the few roles that came his way were unsympathetic—mainly villains and gigolos. *Eyes of Youth* with Clara Kimball Young was far from a masterpiece, but a Hollywood writer named June Mathis caught the 1919 picture and mentally filed this good-looking young fellow away for future reference. While scripting *The Four Horsemen of the Apocalypse* two years later, she insisted on Rudy for the role of Julio in her adaptation of Blasco Ibanez's novel.

The Four Horsemen proved to be the sensation of 1921, and although Valentino appeared responsible for much of the excitement that surrounded the Metro release, he was cast in subsequent pictures as though still a featured player. Upset, and with good reason, Rudy moved over to Paramount at $500 weekly where he was cast as *The Sheik.* This melodramatic tale of love on hot desert sands brought him instant stardom, and While Valentino personally disliked both the film and the role, the combination proved to be a magic which made him the most sought after property on the screen and the object of all kinds of reissues; in those days, if an actor found old pictures in which he had played secondary roles re-released with his name in lights, he realized that the dream had come true—he had finally arrived.

Though most of Valentino's subsequent pictures—*Blood and Sand, Beyond the Rocks, Moran of the Lady Letty, Cobra, The Eagle, Monsieur Beaucaire*—were not extraordinary in themselves, each contained the personality that captivated nearly an entire generation of women (men generally disliked Rudy and his pictures) and despite poor critical reviews and near-constant attack in print by writers with whom he enjoyed less than cordial relations, Valentino's star shone brightly in the mid-twenties.

While Rudy was the epitome of screen sensuality (male gender) for a generation, he was also a bit of an actor in addition to being a box-office draw, and had sufficient integrity to fight his studio every inch of the way about the scripts he was given to play. Much has been made of his private life and especially about the influence of Natasha Rambova, whom he had married, yet Valentino did not abdicate what he felt to be a responsibility to his adoring fans. Natasha certainly captivated the prototype Latin Lover of the screen; but her all-consuming desire to pull the strings that made her husband dance met with periodic resistance, and producers who thought him an easy mark learned that Valentino did have a backbone of his own. He even left the screen to prove his point and returned two years later in *Monsieur Beaucaire*, still a top draw.

The legend that surrounded Valentino's stardom painted him a panting lover whose tango was enough to send any resisting female into spasms of desire, yet few remember that some of Rudy's films were also fast-moving adventure epics in which his superb body and athletic ability lent an air of masculinity to the proceedings. His last, and some feel his best, was a replay of *The Sheik,* entitled appropriately enough *The Son of the Sheik,* and gave the virile lounge lizard an opportunity to combine romance with action and adventure in his final picture. The lounge lizard appelation was a sore point with Rudy; he had been accused many times of being homosexual (less scurrilous attackers were content to hint at this by simply pointing out that he could hardly be heterosexual and let it go at that), and Valentino's on-screen response was an attempt to downplay the smoldering sex appeal by undertaking roles that demanded a he-man approach, few of which he brought off with complete success.

There's little doubt that the critics and detractors who plagued Rudy upset him considerably, and while perhaps they had a point concerning the quality of his films they were most unfair in attacking him personally. Valentino only gave the public what it asked for, and to his credit, he proved most adept at it. More could have been done to exploit the star's capabilities, but none who handled his career were really willing to tamper with success—sex they wanted, sex they got; but boy how the imagination had to fill in the blank spots. Actually, Rudy merely provided the romance; viewers inserted the sex in the privacy of their own minds and his success at hinting should be of interest to those who feel that today's moviegoers are really concerned with seeing everything from beginning to end in the name of reality.

Valentino was a product of the age in which he lived, and historians have often speculated as to how Valentino's career might have gone had it not been for the tragedy of a gallstone operation that proved fatal. There's little doubt in my mind that the Great Lover would have faced the same fate that awaited Jack Gilbert, who lived to see his own career slowly dissipate beneath his capable feet as the vogue that had swept him to the top disappeared. Rudy might well have pushed on into the sound era, but changing public tastes would certainly have ended his reign, regardless of the quality of his voice. And which is a greater burden to carry—death at the peak of a career that insures immortality among the greats of the screen, or the living death of a career which crumbles about the feet of its creator, rendering him a pitiful impotent remnant of a legend destroyed and an era passed by?

Chosen by writer June Mathis to play Julio in The Four Horsemen of the Apocalypse, *Rudolph Valentino was the hit of 1921 in his first major screen role.*

Rudy's portrayal of The Sheik *in 1921 brought him instant adulation;
every woman in America envied Agnes Ayres.*

*Rudy as the young bull fighter whose desire for Nita Naldi temporarily
blinded him to the love of Lila Lee in* Blood and Sand, 1922.

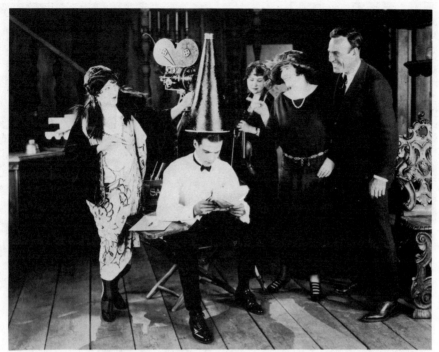

Rudy studies the script as Gloria Swanson cuts up for Elinor Glyn and director Sam Wood on the set of Beyond the Rocks.

But once they settled down for the camera, Gloria and Rudy played like dynamite in a picture unworthy of their talents.

Rudy's reputation as a great lover irked him. After making love to Bebe Daniels, Lois Wilson and Paulette Du Val in Monsieur Beaucaire, *1924 . . .*

. . . Valentino demonstrated his masculinity with action.

Nita Naldi and Cobra, *1926.*

Valentino's next-to-last picture, The Eagle, *1926.*

The Son of the Sheik, *1926.*

HENRY B. WALTHALL

Few actors on the silent screen possessed the capabilities of Henry B. Walthall, yet the fine acting performances of this talented Southern gentleman have received little recognition. A law student who entered the theatre in New York City, he had met with little success when D. W. Griffith brought him to the screen in 1909 as a member of the Biograph's growing stock company. Biograph films at the time were outstanding examples of the movies' ability to move audiences from a lethargic stare to an emotional response, thanks mainly to Griffith and his performers, and Walthall quickly adapted to the new medium.

In a day when theatrical staging and gestures permeated the fare offered the movie public, Walthall's restrained and sensitive portrayals soon made him a popular favorite and he played every conceivable role under the astute director's guidance. As Henry's talents far exceeded the demands that screen acting placed upon him in those days, he emerged from the Biograph period as a notable performer whose lengthy list of screen credits were the envy of many lesser actors. Walthall's years with Griffith were his greatest, despite the fact that he continued to give superior performances well into the thirties.

Much has been made of Griffith's ability to extract creditable performances from minor players whose fame evaporated almost as rapidly as it arrived once they left the director's fold, yet with Henry the roadblocks that appeared in his career were mainly of the actor's own making. Leaving Griffith after *The Birth of a Nation*, Walthall had the misfortune to align his career with organizations like Essanay, whose great days were virtually ended, and despite superb performances in minor classics like *Ghosts* and *The Raven*, even Henry's considerable talents were unable to keep his stature sufficiently high while working for companies whose films played in fewer and fewer theatres each month.

Henry's role as "The Little Colonel" in Griffith's masterpiece was the high point of a lengthy career that lasted another two decades beyond the 1915 classic, and allowed him full opportunity to mix dramatics with romance and heroic action with tender moments. In fact, it's still recognized today as one of the outstanding portrayals in the history of the screen, and as long as prints of *The Birth of a Nation* still circulate, younger generations will have an opportunity to see what screen acting was (and is) all about.

Walthall wasn't a romantic leading man in the fashion of the day, but his face was a changing volcano of emotion; and like Lillian Gish, with whom he often worked at Biograph, Henry was able to convey a variety of emotions with his ever-sad eyes and sensitive pantomime. Unfortunately, his presence on the screen in the twenties was wasted in a succession of unworthy pictures, and it was almost the end of the silent era before he appeared in important roles such as *The Scarlet Letter* and *The Road to Mandalay* at M-G-M. By then, his youth was gone and Walthall's great acting ability could be put to use only in a limited selection of roles.

Never a star of the first magnitude who drew crowds to the box-office on the strength of his own name, Henry was nevertheless a consummate actor who could always be counted on to extract everything from the script, and in some cases even add a little to the writer's efforts. His presence lent dignity and value to everything in which he appeared, yet there are not many fans of the silent screen able to recognize him beyond his performance in *The Birth of a Nation,* and fewer still can name his accomplishments after leaving Griffith.

But his voice was perfect for the talkies and in a succession of supporting parts in major pictures (and even leading roles in lesser productions), Henry B. Walthall came to the fore once more in the early days of sound, working until he died in harness while making *China Clipper,* a 1936 film in which he was to die on-screen. The script had to be changed, as his own death preceded the screen demise. Walthall was one of those actors fortunate enough to share in the shaping of the early motion picture, and in doing so he hastened the development of the "flickers" into an entertainment medium with some semblance of artistic form. Without actors of his calibre, the early screen would have floundered much longer before sensing its direction, and like Frank Keenan at Triangle, Henry never gave a really bad performance—he simply had the misfortune of working in a lot of less-than-memorable pictures which constituted the bulk of screen fare then as now. But regardless of the calibre of the film in which he appeared, the presence of Henry B. Walthall was sufficient to make the picture worth seeing, if only to watch one of the screen's most accomplished craftsmen at work.

Henry B. Walthall.

A Change of Spirit, *1912.*

A member of D. W. Griffith's stock company at Biograph, Walthall played every conceivable role. Here he is as the Assyrian Holofernes, about to be betrayed by Blanche Sweet in Judith of Bethulia, *1914.*

His most moving and best remembered role came as "The Little Colonel" in Griffith's The Birth of a Nation, 1915, *shown here with Lillian Gish.*

As the returned Dr. Prynne, Walthall talks with Governor Tooker in The Scarlet Letter, 1926.

Enjoying the bizarre, Walthall fascinated audiences with his portrayal of Edgar Allan Poe in Essanay's The Raven, 1915.

By the mid-twenties, he was turning to small but interesting portrayals. This was from Lon Chaney's The Road to Mandalay *in 1926.*

BRYANT WASHBURN

While the early screen had many popular heroes who helped to give the movies form and shape, few retained the glamor of stardom into the twenties. Then as now, screen fame was a fleeting crown which retained its lustre but a few years. (The 42-year career of John Wayne, as popular at this writing as he has ever been, is a phenomenon in itself; most actors watch advancing age or declining popularity relegate them to supporting roles or retirement.) But the early stars were very important to the motion picture, and while the star system has been roundly condemned for its many vices and lack of virtue, it played a large role in the growth and popularity of the movies as an entertainment medium.

The popularity of a few stars contributed heavily toward keeping the companies for which they worked alive—Theda Bara and Tom Mix at Fox, Douglas Fairbanks and William S. Hart at Triangle, Francis X. Bushman and Mary Miles Minter at Metro fell into this category. The survival of Essanay into 1917 despite its antiquated outlook and attitudes resulted mainly from the screen efforts of Broncho Billy Anderson, Charlie Chaplin and a Chicago-born socialite named Bryant Washburn.

Franklin Bryant Washburn III had turned to the motion picture in 1911 after his stage career hit a low spot. Acting jobs for him were scarce and only the movies seemed to offer steady employment. Washburn's acting experience had been rather slender, beginning after high school when he joined the Chicago Opera House as head usher. When the cashier proved to be a financial wizard who disappeared one night with the receipts in hand, manager George Kingbury selected Washburn to replace the departed employee, and there he stayed until George Fawcett arrived in *The Great John Ganton.* Leaving his employment with the Opera House to become one of Fawcett's "walking gentlemen," Bryant was paid $1.00 for each performance, which consisted simply of walking on-stage with the star. It wasn't much, but it was a beginning and he did get to dress in white flannels, blazer and straw hat.

The stay with Fawcett led to an engagement in summer stock at Lake

Brady, Ohio, and then to Toronto, where Bryant enjoyed a brief stay with a Canadian stock company. Returning to the United States, he found roles in *The Third Rail* and *The Wolf* at the same time, and a hunch told him to accept the lead in *The Wolf,* which ran for 35 weeks. Although directed by a fellow named Cecil B. DeMille, the other play lasted only a week before the theatre went dark. When *The Wolf* closed, Washburn returned to Chicago where he once again found work with Fawcett in *The Remittance Man,* his final stage work in a four-year career that was anything but memorable. Out of work, Bryant joined Essanay in April 1911 on a ten-week contract that paid $45.00 weekly; he stayed until the firm closed its doors in 1917.

Bryant Washburn played a great variety of roles on the screen in those early days, but while his best portrayals seemed to be as the wealthy idler, there was little specialization during those formative years; this gave actors a chance to play many roles that would be denied them a decade later when type-casting was firmly in control of an actor's destiny. As president of Essanay, George K. Spoor believed in short films and low salaries, and Bryant appeared in countless one- and two-reelers from 1911 to 1915, playing leads, heavies and even walk-ons; his first salary raise came two years after he joined the company. With the extra $5.00 weekly, he married a stage actress, Mabel Forrest.

It was in 1917 feature hits like *Skinner's Dress Suit, Skinner's Baby* and *Skinner Steps Out* (adapted from a popular series of stories by Henry Dodge) that Bryant really scored big, but Spoor continued to keep a close watch on the payroll and when Essanay finally collapsed a few months later, Washburn was earning a mere $200 weekly. Leaving Chicago for Hollywood, he signed with Paramount to play leads at $1000 a week, a sum far closer to his real worth, and soon came into his own with a series of inexpensive but profitable pictures like *Putting It Over, A Very Good Man* and *It Pays to Advertise.*

But Bryant was never to exceed his popularity at Essanay during 1915–17 and after three years with Famous Players, he left to do a few pictures for Pathé before organizing Bryant Washburn Productions to film his own. Like so many actors and actresses who had rushed into business with their own companies between 1917–21, he found that production was a very costly mistake; the screen was filled with handsome leading men looking for work, and Washburn, who had spent far too many years with Essanay to develop a strong, identifiable screen personality, became another casualty of changing audience tastes.

Closing his company, Bryant freelanced throughout the twenties and into the thirties, alternating screen appearances with stage plays and touring companies. Much of his work after disbanding his own company was done for independents—*Temptation* (C.B.C.), *In the First Degree* (Sterling), *Modern Daughters* (Rayart)—and while he worked consistently and turned in creditable performances, time and audience favor had passed him by. A revamping of his 1917 hit character came with *Skinner's Big Idea* for FBO in 1928, but it failed to work the same magic over.

Divorced from Miss Forrest, he married Virginia Vance (a comedienne at Educational) and retired to a quiet life in the Hollywood hills, occasionally picking up parts in a variety of films from *Stagecoach* to *King of the Royal Mounted.* By the time of his death in 1963, few remembered Bryant Washburn's name and still fewer his fame, yet the motion picture owed its popularity over the years to countless actors like Bryant, who had won the hearts and pocketbooks of early audiences with hundreds of delightful performances over the years.

Bryant Washburn.

Bryant and director George Melford.

Here's a rare one—Essanay's idol poses for a studio gag shot with a cockeyed photographer whose fame came at Mack Sennett's Fun Factory as Ben Turpin.

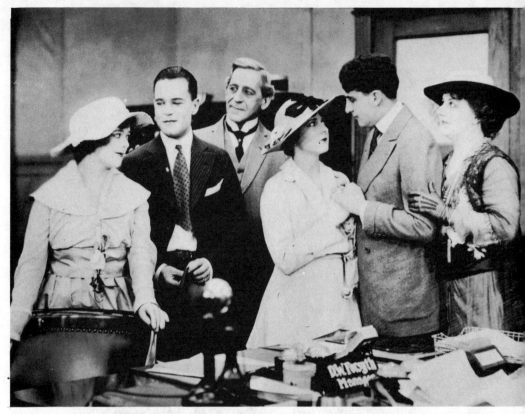

The Spider's Web, 1916. That's John Junior (remember him?) eyeing Betty Burbridge as Bryant and Gertrude Glover make up under the watchful gaze of Florence Oberle. Miss Burbridge enjoyed a long career as a script writer after leaving the screen around World War I.

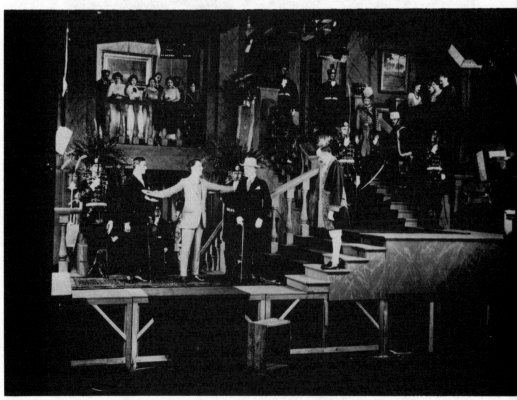

On the set of The Prince of Graustark, one of Bryant's 1916 hits.

Bryant and Richard Travers talk it all over with a few drinks in Filling His Own Shoes, 1917.

An Essanay feature of 1917, Skinner's Baby *was one of Washburn's biggest hits.*

With Florence Vidor in Till I Come Back to You, *1918.*

Full House, *1918.*

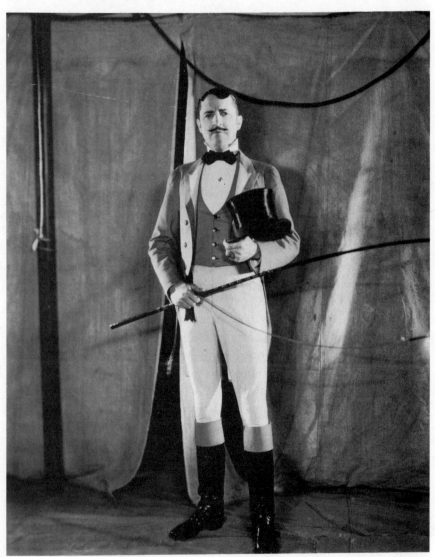

Sound didn't treat Bryant as well as it might have. In Swing High, 1930, Helen Twelvetrees and Fred Scott had the leads; Bryant played the ringmaster.

BEN WILSON

Heroes came and went on the silent screen but some who seemed to have been present when the movies were born appeared to be as indestructible over the years to the fans of their generation as John Wayne is today; one such was a Centerville, Iowa actor named Benjamin Franklin Wilson. Ben, as he preferred to be known, made his first stage appearance in September 1898 and spent the next 12 years in stock, mainly in the New York-Brooklyn-Newark area, before trading live applause for the quiet whir of the Edison camera in 1911. His screen debut came in *For Her Brother's Crime,* a short melodrama that started Ben on the road to becoming one of Edison's top leading men, an achievement that took only a little more than one year.

Tall, well-proportioned and ruggedly handsome, Ben made an ideal hero. His wavy brown hair and piercing eyes gave him a look that women found intriguing and he was chosen to work with Mary Fuller in Edison's two primitive serial efforts of 1912–13, *What Happened to Mary* and *Who Will Marry Mary?* From 1911 through 1917, Ben was constantly on-screen for Edison and Universal, while adding the arts of script writing and direction to his repertoire. Along the way, he unofficially teamed up with a petite brunette actress from Chicago named Neva Gerber and the two became somewhat inseparable companions on-screen.

As an actor, Ben left something to be desired. Although he had a perfect physical appearance for he-man roles, Wilson seemed to have but two moods; an ebullient smile for lighter scenes and a steely-eyed, thoughtful stare for the high dramatic moments. Miss Gerber's range was similarly handicapped but the pair struck gold in 1917 with a Universal serial entitled *The Voice on the Wire* and for the next few years, he and Miss Gerber were weekly visitors on neighborhood theatre screens in one cliffhanger after another.

This extreme popularity as a serial duo proved to be the key that allowed Ben to realize his ambition. Ben turned producer in 1918 on the strength of his box-office draw and went into business for himself, turning out chapter plays in which he and Miss Gerber co-starred for release on the independent market. Between starring in his own serials and producing the Robertson-Cole features made at Universal's studio, Ben was successful enough to buy the recently defunct Bulls Eye Film lot on Santa Monica Boulevard in early 1920, and once *The Screaming Shadow* was completed for Hallmark release he occupied his new studio and set to work.

For the remainder of the silent era, Benjamin Franklin Wilson was one of the most prolific producer-director-actors working in the independent field. Under Berwilla and other corporate names, Ben ground out comedies, serials and melodramas with a rapidity matched only by J. P. McGowan, but unlike that director-writer-actor, Wilson owned the properties and prospered considerably. Ben had given Jack Hoxie's career a large boost by starring him in a group of silent westerns that led the cowboy directly to a Universal contract and several other actors found an association with Ben F. Wilson an asset to their careers.

The majority of Ben's pictures, both those in which he starred and those he produced, were straightforward and uncomplicated in nature, similar to the Republic and Monogram features of the sound era in which potentially explosive dramatic situations were routinely handled in a not-very-subtle way by the use of dialogue; in the case of Ben's silents, by subtitles. Ben had stumbled upon the "B" picture long before that designation came into use, and under his guiding hand the programmer came into its own.

Wilson was not the only producer operating with inexpensive, quickly-produced pictures, but he stands out as one of the most successful and even Universal's assembly line of the twenties had a difficult time matching Wilson's output on a time-cost-return basis. From time to time, Ben even put in an appearance in front of the camera, but his age was showing badly by mid-decade and youthful heroics on his part seemed out of place. Chapter play fans who recall *Officer 444, The Mystery Box* and *The Power God* remember that Ben had slowed down considerably. For Ben, the 1920s were mainly years of promoting and manipulating business deals behind the scenes.

As Wilson's pictures were quickies, their hasty completion was painfully evident to all including the kids, but who can argue with success? Glaring inconsistencies in plotting were typical of the Wilson productions, as were action sequences involving fight scenes that left Boy Scouts roaring in the aisles at the ineptitude shown by rough tough hoodlums and rougher tougher policemen. Crowd scenes in which part of the cast scooted off-screen to the left, around the camera with a change of hats

and back into the picture at the right side of the screen added a touch of
expensive atmosphere and gave the impression of several dozen extras
working a scene at once; Ben may not have been much of an actor or
director but he certainly had a head for business and what brought the
small-town filmgoer into theatres.

Although recalled today primarily for his serial escapades with Neva
Gerber, the influence that Ben F. Wilson exerted on independent production and distribution should not be forgotten; hardly a week passed
in the mid-twenties without his name appearing on the neighborhood
theatre screens in some capacity, and beginning with *The Voice From the
Sky,* a 1929 sound serial starring Wally Wales, he carried on into the
talkies. Of the many who had started practically with the birth of the
movies, few were able to point to careers as prolific and in a sense as
influential as Ben's. A considerable number with more talent had fallen
by the wayside, yet Wilson understood one thing that others underestimated or passed off with a wave of the hand—what audiences really loved
was not art but hokum, and Benjamin Franklin Wilson dealt it out in
large, palatable doses to a responsive public. In today's world of inexpensive independent production of pseudo-realistic films, Ben would probably
be right at home and an even greater success.

Ben Wilson.

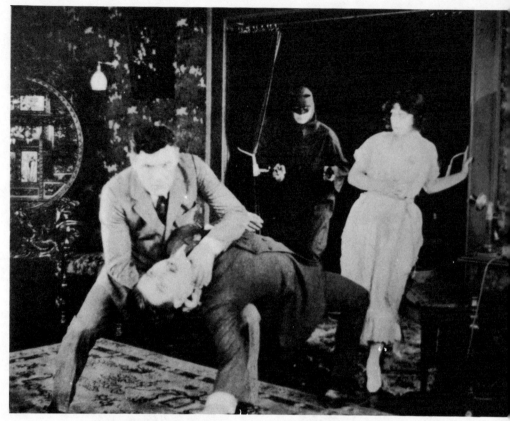

With Neva Gerber in The Branded Four, *1920.*